AF703794

END TIMES ECONOMICS

Money, Faith, and the Future of Civilization

Table of Contents

Introduction 1
Chapter 1 The Myth of Endless Growth 3
The Limits of a Finite Planet 4
The Psychology of Economic Expansion 6
When Growth Becomes a Civilizational Illusion 8
Chapter 2 Collapse as an Economic Pattern 12
Historical Cycles of Rise and Decline 13
Warning Signs Modern Nations Ignore 15
How Systems Fail Quietly Before They Fail All at Once 18
Chapter 3 The Spiritual Roots of Money 21
Faith, Value, and the Human Imagination 22
Sacred Economies of the Ancient World 24
The Moral Weight of Wealth 27
Chapter 4 Digital Currency and the New Global Order 30
The End of Physical Money 31
Central Bank Digital Currencies and Control 33
Economic Power in a Cashless Civilization 36
Chapter 5 Inequality at the Edge of Collapse 39
The Rise of the Ultra-Elite Class 40
The Shrinking Middle and the Desperate Majority 42
Social Erosion in the Age of Extreme Wealth Gaps 45
Chapter 6 Technology, Automation, and the Death of Work 48
When Machines Replace Human Purpose 49
The Social Impact of Permanent Job Disruption 51
The New Aristocracy of Data and Algorithms 54
Chapter 7 Religion, Prophecy, and Economic Fear 57
How Faith Traditions Interpret Crisis 58
Apocalyptic Narratives and Market Psychology 60

The Search for Meaning When Systems Break 63
Chapter 8 Resource Wars and the Economics of Scarcity 66
Water, Energy, and the New Battlegrounds 67
Strategic Scarcity as Political Weaponry 69
Competing Powers in a Depleted World 72
Chapter 9 Surveillance, Control, and the Managed Citizen 75
The Economics of Watching 76
Behavioral Engineering Through Data 78
Power in an Age Without Privacy 81
Chapter 10 The Global Power Shift 84
The Decline of Old Empires 85
The Emergence of New Hegemonies 87
Economic Alliances Reshaping the World 89
Chapter 11 Humanity at the Threshold 93
Ethical Crossroads of the Coming Era 94
The Struggle Between Hope and Despair 96
What Civilization Chooses to Become 98
Chapter 12 Building a Future Beyond Survival 101
Reimagining Prosperity Without Exploitation 102
A New Moral Foundation for Global Systems 104
The Economics of a Post-Collapse World 107

INTRODUCTION

End Times Economics is not a book about doom for the sake of doom. It is an inquiry into the quiet tremors shaping our age—forces that move beneath the surface of daily life, subtle enough to ignore yet powerful enough to redefine the fate of nations. Every civilization believes, in its confident years, that its structures will outlive the storms. But history has a way of humbling even the most ambitious empires, often not through sudden catastrophe but through a gradual erosion of the assumptions that once held everything together.

Today, we live in a world that feels both advanced and strangely fragile. Our economic systems produce extraordinary wealth, yet millions sense an undercurrent of instability—a feeling that something fundamental is shifting, even if they cannot pinpoint where the fault line lies. We see unprecedented technology and convenience, but also widening inequality, anxious markets, and a public losing trust in the institutions meant to guide them. It is this paradox—prosperity and precarity intertwined—that defines the moment we find ourselves in.

Economics, at its core, has always been a story about human behavior, faith, and imagination. Money works only because people believe in it. Nations rise because people trust that their future will be better than their past. Markets thrive because strangers agree to act as if value exists in places where nothing physically stands. Yet when belief falters—when faith in systems, leaders, or narratives collapses—economies unravel faster than any spreadsheet can predict. That intersection between money and belief is the terrain this book explores.

We are entering an era where the old pillars of stability—growth, work, resources, and even shared moral frameworks—are being questioned. The idea of perpetual economic expansion, once taken as gospel, now clashes with ecological limits and technological disruption. Jobs that once anchored identity and social purpose are disappearing into algorithms. Wealth concentrates at the top while the majority struggles to hold ground. Governments race to control digital currencies, data, and behavior, aware that whoever commands these tools commands the future. And beneath it all is a recurring human impulse: to interpret crisis through the lens of prophecy, destiny, or moral reckoning.

This book does not claim that civilization is destined to collapse. Rather, it argues that we have reached a point where ignoring deep structural vulnerabilities is no longer an option. The signs are visible in global markets, environmental degradation, political extremism, and the quiet loneliness of people who feel economically abandoned. These patterns are not random. They follow historical precedents, psychological truths, and spiritual questions that humanity has grappled with for centuries.

End Times Economics invites the reader to step back from the noise of headlines and consider the larger forces shaping the future—forces that align economics with faith, technology with morality, and individual choices with civilizational outcomes. The coming decades will test not only our institutions, but our imagination and courage. This book is a guide to understanding the world we are building, whether consciously or by default, and the world that may emerge when the old assumptions finally meet their limits.

CHAPTER 1

THE MYTH OF ENDLESS GROWTH

The Myth of Endless Growth begins with a question that modern society rarely pauses to ask: How long can a civilization expand before it encounters the boundaries of the world that sustains it? For decades, politicians, economists, and corporate leaders have spoken as if growth were a law of nature—an unstoppable upward line on a chart, immune to the limits that govern everything else in existence. Yet beneath that confident narrative lies a truth both simple and unsettling: we live on a finite planet, and no system can grow forever without consequence.

The belief in perpetual growth is more than an economic ideal; it is a cultural story that has shaped modern identity. Nations measure success through GDP, businesses through quarterly expansion, and individuals through rising incomes or assets. Growth promises security, progress, and relevance. It tells people that tomorrow will reward their effort more generously than today. That psychological comfort is powerful, and it fuels the engine of consumption, innovation, and ambition.

But when a society becomes dependent on expansion for stability, it begins to fear the very idea of slowing down. A plateau is treated like a crisis; a decline, like a moral failure. Growth transforms from a practical goal into a sacred expectation, a symbol of national pride and personal hope. Over time, the numbers on the charts begin to matter more than the realities they're meant to represent—environmental strain, human exhaustion, political tension, and the quiet recognition that exponential growth on a constrained Earth is mathematically impossible.

This chapter explores how the pursuit of endless expansion became a civilizational myth—one so deeply woven into modern life that questioning it feels almost radical. It examines the physical limits of our planet, the psychological forces that make growth addictive, and the illusions that form when a society refuses to imagine alternatives.

The Limits of a Finite Planet

Every era inherits a set of unquestioned assumptions that shape how people think, behave, and plan for the future. For the modern world, one of the most deeply embedded assumptions is that economic growth can continue indefinitely. We speak about expansion as though it were a natural law—an upward trajectory that, with enough innovation and determination, will always push further. Yet when we step back from the abstractions of economic theory and look directly at the physical world, a very different reality comes into focus. Earth is not an infinite canvas. It is a closed, bounded system with measurable limits, and our pursuit of perpetual expansion increasingly collides with the constraints of that system.

The planet's natural resources—its forests, minerals, freshwater, fertile soils, and energy reserves—form the backbone of human civilization. Every industry, every city, every technological breakthrough ultimately rests on these foundational materials. But they do not replenish at the speed our economies demand. Forests regenerate slowly, soils recover over decades, and fossil fuels take millions of years to form. When extraction intensifies to serve an expanding global population and a consumption-driven economic model, nature struggles to keep pace. The consequences are visible: deforestation that alters climate patterns, fisheries depleted to the brink of collapse, and aquifers drained faster than they can refill. These are not abstract warnings; they are the early symptoms of a civilization pressing against planetary boundaries.

Climate change is perhaps the most striking manifestation of this tension. Industrial growth has been fueled by carbon-rich energy sources that release greenhouse gases into the atmosphere. For decades, the atmosphere absorbed this output quietly. But the capacity of any system to absorb waste is finite. Today, rising temperatures, melting ice sheets, and extreme weather patterns reveal that the Earth is no longer buffering our emissions without consequence. The planet is signaling that the margin for unchecked expansion has narrowed dramatically. What was once an economic question has become an existential one: How long can a growth-dependent system survive when its foundational conditions are destabilizing?

Water scarcity deepens the problem. Freshwater—so essential it is often taken for granted—exists in limited supply, unevenly distributed across the globe. Many of the world's major rivers no longer reach the sea during certain seasons because they are siphoned off for agriculture and urban use. Aquifers, which should serve as long-term reserves, are collapsing under the pressure of over-extraction. Countries that once assumed water abundance now face seasonal shortages and rising geopolitical tension over shared sources. Economic expansion has multiplied demand, but the planet's hydrological cycle does not accelerate simply because human economies require it to.

Food production faces similar constraints. Modern agriculture, driven by the imperative of feeding billions, relies heavily on fertilizers, irrigation, and monoculture systems. These methods temporarily boost yield but degrade long-term soil health. Nutrient depletion, erosion, and salinization silently erode the foundation of the global food supply. As soil quality declines, more land must be cleared, creating a self-reinforcing cycle of environmental strain. Once again, the contradiction becomes evident: a model that demands constant output rests on systems that need rest, regeneration, and balance.

Even the idea of innovation as a limitless escape route reveals its limits under scrutiny. Technology can increase efficiency and unlock new resources, but it cannot rewrite the laws of thermodynamics. Every process produces waste; every new material requires extraction; every digital network depends on physical infrastructure. Solutions often shift pressure from one system to another—reducing emissions in one sector while increasing mineral demand in another. Human ingenuity is remarkable, but it cannot conjure infinite supply from a finite world.

The deeper issue is not merely resource scarcity but the psychological and cultural framework that normalizes the pursuit of "more." Modern civilization treats consumption as a proxy for progress and expansion as synonymous with success. That mindset blinds us to the ecological reality that growth must eventually encounter constraint. The more we stretch these limits, the more destabilizing the consequences become—economic volatility, mass displacement, political conflict, and social unrest. These pressures do not emerge suddenly; they accumulate quietly until they reach a breaking point.

And so, the limits of a finite planet are not simply environmental boundaries. They are civilizational boundaries. They force us to confront a truth we have avoided: that no society can expand perpetually without eventually overwhelming the systems that sustain it. The Earth is generous but not boundlessly so. Its cycles can support abundance, but only when human ambition respects ecological equilibrium. As long as our economic narrative ignores this truth, we drift closer to a future shaped by depletion rather than prosperity.

Recognizing planetary limits is not an admission of defeat. It is the beginning of a more honest conversation about what a sustainable, meaningful economy might look like—one built not on endless extraction, but on balance, resilience, and respect for the world that makes civilization possible.

The Psychology of Economic Expansion

Every economic system is built not only on resources, labor, and policy, but on something far more fragile and far more powerful: human psychology. Beneath every chart, currency, or market cycle lies a network of beliefs, emotions, and expectations that shape how societies behave. The drive for economic expansion—so deeply woven into modern life—did not emerge merely from industrial capability or technological progress. It grew from the human mind's desire for security, meaning, and upward momentum. Growth feels natural to us because it mirrors the way we imagine our own lives should unfold: moving forward, improving, expanding. When growth slows, we interpret it as failure, not simply as a change in state.

From childhood, many people in modern societies are raised inside narratives of progress. They are taught to dream bigger, aim higher, and measure personal fulfillment in terms of advancement. Nations absorb the same psychology. A rising GDP becomes a symbol of collective achievement. More production means more jobs, more choices, more confidence. Economic expansion reassures people that tomorrow will be better than today, and that the sacrifices they make now will eventually lead to reward. Growth functions as a psychological stabilizer; when people believe the future is expanding, they tolerate present discomfort, invest in long-term plans, and trust institutions more readily.

At its core, economic expansion taps into a universal human desire: the fear of scarcity and the longing for abundance. For most of human history, survival depended on hoarding, storing, and preparing for uncertain seasons. Even in the modern era, with its abundance of goods, the old instinct remains etched into our behavior. Societies seek growth partly to outrun the ancient anxiety that there may not be enough. When economies expand, people feel safer. When they stagnate, even briefly, latent fears resurface—fears that wealth may disappear, opportunities may shrink, and lives may unravel.

This emotional undercurrent shapes policy and politics as much as rational economic calculation. Leaders promise growth because citizens instinctively crave it. Businesses pursue expansion because shareholders equate it with vitality. Entire political agendas rise and fall on the promise of stimulating the economy. Rarely do people ask whether the expansion is sustainable or beneficial at a deeper level; the psychological reward of upward movement overwhelms more cautious reasoning. Growth becomes a cultural expectation, not just an economic goal.

Yet this expectation contains a hidden paradox. The more a society depends on expansion for psychological stability, the more vulnerable it becomes to any sign of slowdown. When growth falters—even slightly—fear spreads quickly. Markets react not only to data but to sentiment. Consumer confidence drops, investment stalls, and institutions face scrutiny. A self-reinforcing cycle emerges: fear of decline triggers behaviors that make decline more likely. In this way, the psychology of expansion becomes the psychology of fragility. The belief in endless upward motion sets the stage for panic when the upward motion inevitably pauses.

Much of this behavior stems from cognitive biases that humans carry unconsciously. One of the most powerful is the extrapolation bias—the assumption that current trends will continue into the future. When the economy grows, people assume it will keep growing. When housing prices rise, buyers believe they will always rise. When technology accelerates, societies assume the acceleration is permanent. This bias leads people to underappreciate risk, underestimate limits, and overvalue future rewards. Expansion becomes not just desirable but expected.

Another key factor is social comparison. Humans instinctively measure their well-being relative to others. Expansion feeds this dynamic by offering constant opportunities to improve one's position. People do not simply want more; they want more than before, and ideally more than others around them. This constant upward comparison fuels consumption, competition, and pressure to keep the economy swelling. Stagnation threatens not just financial outcomes but personal identity, because individuals embed their sense of worth in the ability to progress.

At a collective level, growth also creates a psychological narrative of purpose. Societies anchored in expansion believe they are moving toward something—a bigger economy, a stronger nation, a better life. When expansion slows, meaning itself feels disrupted. People begin to ask harder questions: What is the purpose of our economy? What is the purpose of work? What is the purpose of progress? These existential concerns reveal that economic expansion is not only a financial mechanism but a cultural myth that offers direction and coherence.

But no myth can sustain itself indefinitely when it clashes with physical limits, demographic shifts, or environmental strain. As the planet pushes back against constant extraction and markets confront structural constraints, societies must face the psychological discomfort of imagining a future where expansion is no longer guaranteed. The transition is difficult not because alternative economic models are impossible, but because they challenge deep emotional patterns—our instinctive need for "more," our fear of "less," and our belief that progress must always accelerate.

Understanding the psychology of expansion is essential for navigating the centuries ahead. If civilization hopes to adapt, it must learn to decouple well-being from perpetual growth, redefine progress in more meaningful terms, and cultivate resilience rather than dependence on constant upward motion. Only then can humanity confront the future with clarity rather than fear.

When Growth Becomes a Civilizational Illusion

For most of the modern era, economic growth has been presented not merely as a desirable outcome but as an unquestionable truth—a force as natural as gravity and as inevitable as the rising sun. Governments campaign on promises of expansion, corporations structure their identities around perpetual scaling, and individuals internalize the belief that progress must always accelerate. Growth, in this sense, becomes a civilizational narrative: a shared illusion so familiar and comforting that people rarely pause to examine its foundations. Yet illusions, no matter how compelling, eventually collide with reality. And when growth becomes an illusion, civilizations begin to drift into dangerous territory.

The illusion begins with abstraction. Economic indicators—GDP, productivity rates, stock indices—are treated as proxies for well-being. As long as these numbers rise, society presumes it is becoming healthier, richer, and more stable. These metrics, however, are simplified representations of complex systems. They measure output, not sustainability; activity, not health. A country may increase GDP by cutting forests, depleting fisheries, or overworking its labor force, but those costs remain hidden behind the comforting upward slope of growth charts. The illusion persists because the symbols of progress remain positive even as the underlying structures weaken.

This disconnect gains momentum through technological innovation. Modern societies often believe that technology can outpace any limit or compensate for any scarcity. When energy runs short, new extraction techniques appear. When materials grow scarce, substitutes seem to emerge. When pollution increases, filters and regulations offer partial relief. Innovation becomes a kind of secular salvation narrative—one that promises humanity can continue expanding indefinitely if it is clever enough. But technology, for all its brilliance, cannot erase the fundamental truth that Earth has finite capacity. It can delay constraints, shift burdens, or mask damage, but it cannot create infinite resources out of nothing.

The illusion of perpetual growth is further reinforced by the structure of global finance. Debt-based economies rely on the assumption of future expansion to remain functional. Loans are issued based on the belief that tomorrow's economy will be large enough to pay for today's borrowing. Entire financial systems spiral outward from this assumption. When growth slows, the financial architecture begins to crack. This fragility means societies have powerful psychological and institutional incentives to maintain the illusion, even when evidence suggests the foundation is eroding. Acknowledging limits becomes threatening because it challenges the solvency of nations, corporations, and households alike.

Psychologically, people cling to the myth because it provides emotional security. Growth promises opportunity, stability, and rising living standards. It tells parents that their children will live better than they did. It gives workers a reason to tolerate long hours, students a reason to invest in education, and entrepreneurs a reason to take risks. When growth falters, so does the sense of future possibility. Anxiety rises, trust in institutions erodes, and political extremism gains traction. In this way, the illusion of endless growth becomes a stabilizing myth—one that civilizations use to maintain social cohesion.

But illusions have consequences. When societies behave as though limits do not exist, they inevitably push beyond what their environments, economies, and social structures can bear. This often manifests as overconsumption of resources, extreme inequality, and unsustainable urban expansion. The promise of continued growth encourages speculative bubbles—housing, tech, finance—that inflate rapidly and burst catastrophically. Each cycle becomes more destabilizing than the last, because the underlying illusion grows more fragile while the real constraints become sharper.

Environmental degradation is perhaps the most visible symptom of this illusion. From collapsing fisheries to disappearing glaciers, the natural world responds to human expansion with clear signals. Yet these warnings are often dismissed or minimized because they contradict the growth narrative. Governments and corporations hesitate to make meaningful changes because doing so would require confronting the myth directly. The result is a collective denial: a quiet, almost subconscious refusal to accept that the old model of progress cannot continue.

A more subtle consequence emerges in the moral landscape. When growth becomes the ruling myth, human values often shift toward efficiency, competition, and accumulation at the expense of community, balance, and restraint. People begin to measure their worth through productivity rather than character, consumption rather than contribution.

Societies become restless, always chasing the next achievement, the next expansion, the next breakthrough. The illusion shapes behavior not only economically but spiritually, drawing people away from deeper questions about meaning and purpose.

Eventually, reality asserts itself. The limits of ecosystems, the volatility of global markets, and the rising psychological toll of constant acceleration converge into a moment of reckoning. Civilizations that cannot adapt—those that cling desperately to the illusion—risk collapse or fragmentation. Those that face the truth, however difficult, open the door to transformation. Recognizing the illusion is not about embracing decline; it is about redefining progress in a way that aligns with the planet's boundaries and humanity's deeper needs.

When growth becomes a civilizational illusion, the task is not to mourn the endings it forces, but to imagine the beginnings it makes possible. Only by acknowledging the limits we have long ignored can we build a future grounded not in illusions, but in resilience, balance, and wisdom.

CHAPTER 2
COLLAPSE AS AN ECONOMIC PATTERN

Collapse is often imagined as a sudden, dramatic event—a moment when everything breaks at once. In reality, economic collapse tends to unfold slowly, almost imperceptibly, as a series of subtle shifts that accumulate over decades. Civilizations rarely fall because of a single catastrophe. They fall because their internal structures weaken quietly while their leaders, institutions, and citizens convince themselves that the familiar patterns of stability will continue indefinitely. This chapter explores collapse not as an anomaly, but as a recurring economic pattern woven throughout human history.

Every great society has believed, at its height, that it had finally escaped the cycles that destroyed those before it. The Romans, the Mayans, the Ottomans, the British Empire—each assumed its system was exceptional, immune to the forces that had toppled earlier powers. Yet across time and geography, civilizations exhibit strikingly similar trajectories: rapid expansion, institutional overconfidence, growing inequality, environmental strain, and political polarization. By the time collapse becomes visible, the underlying foundations have already been eroded.

Modern nations are no different. Technology, globalization, and financial engineering have created the illusion that today's world is too complex, too interconnected, or too advanced to fail as earlier societies did. But complexity does not grant immunity; it simply changes the shape of vulnerability. The systems that feel strongest are often the most fragile because they depend on assumptions—endless growth, cheap resources, global cooperation—that cannot be guaranteed indefinitely.

This chapter examines three interlocking dimensions: the historical cycles of rise and decline, the warning signs contemporary nations habitually ignore, and the mechanisms through which systems fail quietly before collapsing suddenly. Understanding these patterns is essential, not because collapse is inevitable, but because recognizing its early signals allows societies to adapt before the breaking point arrives.

Historical Cycles of Rise and Decline

Every civilization begins with a spark—an idea, a resource, a moment of unity—that propels it from obscurity into influence. Yet the story of civilization is not linear; it is cyclical. Empires rise, flourish, fragment, and eventually fall, leaving behind ruins, lessons, and unanswered questions. What makes these cycles especially compelling is how consistently they repeat across different eras, continents, and cultures. While the particulars change—technology, language, political structures—the underlying patterns remain strikingly similar. Studying these cycles is not an exercise in nostalgia; it is a way to understand the trajectory of modern nations that may believe themselves immune to history's rhythm.

Historians have long observed that societies tend to move through identifiable stages. The first is the phase of ascent, marked by innovation, unity, and shared purpose. In this phase, resources are abundant or newly discovered, and populations are motivated by a sense of opportunity. The early Roman Republic exemplified this stage, as did the Abbasid Caliphate and the early dynasties of China. These societies expanded their influence rapidly because they were energized by clarity of identity and aligned interests. People felt connected to something larger than themselves, and this cohesion translated into economic growth, social stability, and political agility.

The next stage is maturity, when a civilization reaches its peak. Institutions become sophisticated, infrastructure expands, and cultural achievements flourish. This is the moment when societies often mistake strength for permanence. The Ming Dynasty's monumental projects, the Ottoman Empire's administrative reforms, and Britain's industrial dominance all exemplified the confidence of maturity. Yet beneath that confidence lies the beginning of fragility. Success can breed complacency. Leaders assume that what worked before will continue to work indefinitely. Systems become rigid and resistant to change. And slowly, often invisibly, the seeds of decline take root.

Decline rarely begins with catastrophe. Instead, it emerges as a gradual erosion of vitality. Resources that once seemed plentiful become strained. Inequality widens, fueling resentment among the lower classes and competition among elites. Public institutions, once efficient and trusted, grow corrupt or ineffective. The Roman Empire, for example, struggled with economic stagnation long before its political collapse. The Mayans faced environmental degradation decades before their cities were abandoned. The British Empire began losing strategic and economic advantages well before its formal dismantling. Decline is not a moment; it is a process—one that leaders often refuse to acknowledge because it contradicts the myth of continuous progress.

Another common feature of decline is overextension. Civilizations frequently expand beyond their capacity to sustain themselves, whether through military campaigns, global trade networks, or administrative complexity. The Mongol Empire, despite its extraordinary reach, fractured under the weight of managing vast territories with limited communication infrastructure. The Spanish Empire, enriched temporarily by New World silver, succumbed to inflation and political overreach. Overextension weakens internal stability because it diverts resources from essential functions to costly ambitions. A society spread too thin cannot easily respond to emerging challenges.

As decline deepens, societies enter a period of fragmentation. The unified identity that once drove ascent gives way to factionalism. Competing interests—economic, political, religious—fight for influence, weakening the cohesion needed to navigate crises. The late Roman Empire suffered from power struggles between generals, politicians, and regional leaders. The Ottoman Empire's later centuries were marked by internal divisions that paralyzed reform efforts. Even technologically advanced societies are vulnerable to this dynamic; when trust erodes, institutions fail to function effectively, regardless of their sophistication.

Eventually, the cycle culminates in collapse. This is the moment historians record most vividly, but it is merely the endpoint of slow deterioration. Collapse may take the form of invasion, economic implosion, environmental catastrophe, or internal revolution. The specific trigger varies, but the result is the same: the system can no longer sustain itself. Yet collapse is rarely total destruction. More often, it is a transformation—a shedding of old structures, a contraction that allows something new to emerge. Post-Roman Europe reorganized into feudal kingdoms. Post-imperial China rebuilt through successive dynasties. After the fall of the Soviet Union, new economic and political systems arose from the remnants.

Why do societies follow this pattern so consistently? Part of the answer lies in human nature. The qualities that drive ascent—ambition, unity, innovation—fade when comfort replaces struggle. The leaders who inherit mature societies often lack the urgency of their predecessors. Institutions become more focused on preserving power than on adapting to change. And populations accustomed to prosperity can resist reforms that require sacrifice. The arc of rise and decline emerges not from external forces alone, but from internal dynamics that gradually undermine resilience.

Modern nations, despite advanced technologies and global interconnectedness, inhabit the same cyclical framework. The belief that our era is uniquely immune to history's patterns is itself a hallmark of civilizations nearing maturity or decline. The lesson of historical cycles is not that collapse is inevitable, but that ignoring early signs increases the likelihood of crisis. Understanding these cycles offers a chance—not to escape history, but to navigate it with humility, awareness, and foresight.

Warning Signs Modern Nations Ignore

Every civilization approaching decline leaves behind a trail of warning signs—patterns so consistent across history that they almost form a universal script. Yet modern nations, armed with data, technology, and unprecedented access to information, often overlook these signs with the same blindness that doomed earlier empires. The assumption that "this time is different" becomes a psychological shield, allowing leaders and citizens alike to ignore evidence that their systems are drifting toward instability. The warnings are rarely subtle, but they are easy to dismiss because acknowledging them requires confronting uncomfortable truths about power, inequality, and the limits of national ambition.

One of the clearest warning signs is widening economic inequality. When a nation's wealth pools at the top while the majority struggles to maintain basic stability, it signals more than an economic malfunction—it reveals deep institutional imbalance. Historically, societies with extreme wealth gaps experience declining social cohesion, rising resentment, and eventually political upheaval. Rome's late republic, the French ancien régime, and the British Empire at its peak all suffered from stratification that hollowed out their middle classes. Modern nations face similar fractures. As the cost of living rises faster than wages and opportunities concentrate in elite networks, resentment becomes widespread. A society cannot maintain unity when its prosperity is experienced by only a fraction of its citizens.

A second warning sign is institutional decay. Nations in decline often experience a deterioration of trust in their governing bodies, legal systems, and public institutions. This erosion does not happen overnight. It begins when corruption becomes normalized, when accountability weakens, and when public offices serve private interests more reliably than the common good. Over time, institutions lose their ability to solve problems, enforce laws fairly, or respond to crises effectively. The public becomes cynical, disengaged, or rebellious. Even technologically advanced societies are not immune; institutional decay is a psychological and moral process before it becomes a structural one.

Environmental disregard is another critical warning. Civilizations throughout history have collapsed after exhausting the natural systems that supported them. The Mayans over-farmed their lands; Mesopotamian cities salinated their soil; Easter Island depleted its forests. Modern nations face environmental pressures on a scale no previous society has confronted: climate instability, water scarcity, biodiversity collapse, and melting ice reserves. Yet many leaders continue to treat environmental warnings as abstract future concerns rather than immediate threats to stability. A nation that erodes its ecological foundation weakens every pillar of its economy, from agriculture to infrastructure to public health.

Political polarization is similarly dangerous. When societies split into hostile ideological camps, the ability to compromise evaporates. Governance becomes paralyzed, not because solutions are unavailable, but because factions prioritize defeating one another over solving problems. Polarization corrodes trust, encourages extremism, and creates openings for demagogues who exploit fear and grievance. Late-stage Rome, the final years of the Weimar Republic, and countless other societies experienced intense polarization before collapse. Modern nations often ignore this warning because political division feels like a sign of freedom or democratic vitality. In reality, when disagreement hardens into tribal identity, a society loses its capacity to function.

Another overlooked sign is overextension—economic, military, or administrative. Nations often stretch themselves beyond their sustainable capacity in pursuit of influence or security. Empires historically expanded until their logistical burdens outweighed their benefits. Today, overextension may appear in the form of national debt, sprawling military commitments, fragile supply chains, or overly complex bureaucratic systems. When a nation becomes dependent on perpetual expansion to maintain stability, it becomes vulnerable to shocks. A modest downturn, a geopolitical shift, or a technological disruption can trigger cascading failures.

Cultural fatigue also plays a role. Civilizations entering decline often lose a sense of shared purpose. Creativity slows, institutions become repetitive rather than innovative, and public life becomes saturated with cynicism. People retreat into individualism or escapism. The collective imagination shrinks. This is not merely a cultural phenomenon—it affects economic productivity, political engagement, and social resilience. Societies without a unifying narrative struggle to mobilize in the face of crisis.

Finally, nations ignore the warning signs of technological overreliance. As systems become more interconnected and automated, they grow more efficient but also more fragile. A single disruption—cyberattacks, supply-chain breaks, infrastructural failure—can ripple across entire economies. Complexity can become a liability when a system's interdependence prevents it from adapting quickly or absorbing shocks.

Taken together, these warning signs form a pattern modern nations often choose not to see. They assume that economic sophistication or military strength grants immunity from historical repetition. But decline rarely begins with dramatic events. It begins with small fractures—ignored, dismissed, normalized—until the accumulated weight becomes too great to bear. The challenge for contemporary societies is not merely to identify these signs, but to act on them before they harden into irreversible trajectories. Recognizing danger early is the only way to avoid repeating the fate of civilizations that once believed themselves unbreakable.

How Systems Fail Quietly Before They Fail All at Once

Civilizations rarely collapse with the kind of sudden drama that popular imagination prefers. More often, systems fail the way a shoreline erodes—grain by grain, tide after tide—until one day a single wave arrives and the land gives way. To outsiders, it looks abrupt; to anyone paying attention, the collapse was merely the final expression of pressures long ignored. Understanding how systems fail quietly is essential, because the quiet phase is where the danger grows and where the opportunity for intervention still exists.

The first stage of quiet failure begins when early signs of strain appear but are interpreted as temporary or manageable. A country faces mild inflation, a slowdown in productivity, or an uptick in political division. Leaders reassure the public that these disruptions are part of normal cycles. Institutions release reports projecting future stability. Citizens continue with daily routines. The system absorbs the stress, but not without cost. Like a bridge carrying traffic beyond its engineered capacity, small cracks form—hidden from plain sight yet progressively weakening the structure.

As these cracks widen, the second stage emerges: normalization of dysfunction. Problems that once seemed alarming become routine. Government deficits grow every year, but citizens acclimate. Infrastructure decays gradually, but repairs are postponed until "next year." Courts become slower, hospitals more crowded, schools underfunded, yet the public adjusts expectations downward. Decline becomes part of the background noise of civic life. A quiet cultural shift takes place: people learn to tolerate what they once would have resisted. This normalization is especially dangerous because it dulls society's capacity for alarm, making systemic instability appear ordinary.

During this stage, feedback loops begin to fail. Healthy systems rely on transparent signals—accurate data, honest journalism, competent oversight—to detect problems early. But in failing systems, these signals distort. Governments may manipulate statistics to appear strong. Corporations may conceal financial risks beneath layers of accounting. Media outlets may polarize narratives rather than illuminate issues. As transparency weakens, decision-makers operate in partial darkness, unable to perceive the true scale of emerging threats. Problems that could have been corrected with moderate intervention now deepen into structural vulnerabilities.

The third stage of quiet failure arrives when interdependence becomes fragility. Modern societies are interconnected to a degree unprecedented in history. Global supply chains, financial systems, energy grids, and digital networks form intricate webs where one failure can trigger another. This complexity creates efficiency but sacrifices resilience. A small disruption—a port shutdown, a cyberattack, a drought—can cascade through multiple sectors. A system that appears stable on the surface may in fact be tightly wound, brittle, and vulnerable to shocks. Quiet failure often thrives in these hidden interdependencies, where weaknesses go unnoticed until they intersect.

Compounding these vulnerabilities is a psychological dimension: denial becomes the default response. Leaders avoid unpopular reforms because the costs are immediate while the benefits are distant. Citizens resist acknowledging decline because doing so threatens their sense of identity and future. Institutions cling to outdated models because changing course requires admitting previous strategies were flawed. This denial accelerates decay by preventing adaptation. The system becomes a machine running outdated software—functional enough to continue operating, but increasingly misaligned with reality.

Eventually, the final stage arrives: the tipping point. This is the moment when the accumulated stress overwhelms the system's ability to absorb it. Financial markets seize after years of hidden leverage. Healthcare systems collapse under the weight of chronic underfunding. Political institutions gridlock until governance becomes impossible. The triggering event may appear sudden—a protest, a drought, a bank failure—but the true cause lies in decades of quiet erosion. When collapse arrives, it feels instantaneous because the public sees only the final break, not the long period of strain that came before.

This phenomenon—known as "failure by accumulation"—explains why societies often describe collapse as shocking, even though historians later identify its inevitability. The quiet phase masks the danger by dispersing it across time. People adapt to gradual deterioration, assuming the system remains stable because it has not yet failed completely. But stability is not endurance; it is merely the period before thresholds are crossed.

Recognizing the stages of quiet failure offers a chance for change. Systems can recover if weaknesses are acknowledged early, if institutions remain honest, and if societies cultivate resilience rather than complacency. The challenge is psychological as much as structural: to resist the temptation of denial, to recognize decline while solutions are still possible, and to understand that collapse is not a single event but a long process that becomes visible only at the end.

Civilizations do not fall all at once. They fail quietly, subtly, predictably—until the moment they don't.

CHAPTER 3

THE SPIRITUAL ROOTS OF MONEY

Money is often described in technical terms—currency, exchange, markets, systems—but beneath its surface lies something far older and far more human. Long before coins, banks, or digital transactions existed, communities relied on shared beliefs to assign value to objects, rituals, and promises. At its core, money is not merely an economic instrument; it is a spiritual construct, born from humanity's capacity to imagine, trust, and agree on symbolic meaning. It requires collective faith to function. Without belief, even the most sophisticated financial system collapses into nothing more than paper, metal, or numbers on a screen.

This chapter explores the spiritual roots of money, not in a religious sense alone, but in the broader realm of human imagination—the place where meaning is created and sustained. Civilizations across history treated wealth as more than a practical tool: they associated it with divine favor, cosmic order, or moral responsibility. From the temples of Mesopotamia to the ceremonial economies of Indigenous tribes, value was intertwined with spirituality, social harmony, and the unseen forces believed to govern prosperity.

The modern world often assumes it has outgrown these ancient conceptions, yet contemporary economies still rely on belief as deeply as any temple-based system. Markets rise and fall on sentiment. Currencies strengthen or weaken based on collective confidence. Nations maintain stability because people agree, often unconsciously, to trust the symbols that represent value. Money remains a shared story that requires constant psychological and moral reinforcement.

This chapter examines three dimensions of these spiritual foundations: the imaginative leap that makes value possible, the sacred economic systems that shaped early civilizations, and the moral weight wealth continues to carry. By understanding the spiritual origins of money, we gain insight into why modern economies behave as they do—and why financial systems remain vulnerable when collective belief weakens.

Faith, Value, and the Human Imagination

Before money becomes a coin, a note, or a digital entry, it begins as a belief. At the heart of every economic system lies an invisible agreement—a shared conviction that something holds value because we collectively decide it does. This agreement is not enforced by nature; it is crafted by the human imagination and sustained by faith. Without that faith, money collapses instantly, regardless of how elaborate the financial institutions surrounding it may be. Understanding this psychological and spiritual foundation is essential for understanding why modern economies behave the way they do.

Human beings are unique in their ability to create meaning through shared stories. Nations, laws, markets, and currencies all function because people believe in them together. Money is one of the clearest expressions of this capacity. A piece of paper has no intrinsic worth. A digital token is only a pattern of information. Even gold, often treated as inherently valuable, is only precious because societies have agreed that its scarcity and beauty make it significant. In reality, money works because humans are capable of forming collective myths—stories that transform ordinary objects into vessels of trust and exchange.

This imaginative leap is ancient. Early societies imbued economic exchange with spiritual significance. Value was intertwined with rituals of offering, gratitude, and cosmic order. Grain stored in temple complexes, livestock exchanged in ceremonies, and shells used as currency were not merely practical tools; they were symbols of communal trust. Giving, receiving, and storing wealth were actions embedded in a moral and spiritual context. People believed their prosperity was tied to divine favor, ancestral guidance, or cosmic balance. The imagination, in this sense, was not escapist—it shaped the material world by defining what people valued and why.

Modern economies often claim to be purely rational systems governed by mathematics and market logic. Yet even today, value is shaped far more by imagination than by physical reality. Stock markets rise on optimism and plunge on fear. Currencies strengthen or weaken largely due to sentiment about national stability. The very concept of "credit"—from the Latin *credere*, meaning "to believe"—reveals that lending is an act of faith in another's future ability to repay. Investors, governments, and consumers engage in rituals of trust every day, echoing the ancient belief that prosperity emerges from shared conviction.

The psychological dimension of value creation becomes especially clear during financial crises. When collective faith fractures, money loses its power almost overnight. Bank runs occur not because vaults are empty, but because people fear they might be. Currency collapses when citizens no longer trust their government to uphold value. In these moments, the spiritual roots of money become unmistakable: value exists only as long as people believe in the story behind it. Once that belief erodes, no amount of technical management can fully restore stability until trust is rebuilt.

The imagination also influences the moral meaning attached to wealth. Cultures throughout history have debated whether wealth signifies virtue, divine blessing, personal effort, or exploitation. These interpretations shape how societies distribute resources and reward labor. If wealth is seen as a sign of cosmic favor, inequality becomes morally justified. If it is viewed as a social contract, citizens expect fairness and accountability. If it is perceived as something dangerous or corrupting, societies regulate or morally restrain accumulation. In each case, imagination shapes not only what money *is*, but what it *means*.

Even consumer behavior reflects this imaginative and spiritual element. People do not merely buy goods for utility; they buy symbols—status, identity, aspiration. A brand becomes valuable because of the story attached to it. An economy thrives not because everyone needs more things, but because people imagine better versions of themselves through consumption. This is a modern form of ritual, no less symbolic than ancient offerings. The marketplace becomes a space where identity is constructed, desires are shaped, and emotions become intertwined with economic choices.

The connection between faith and value also reveals why financial systems are deeply vulnerable. Because value rests on belief, it can dissolve more quickly than physical resources can. A rumor can destabilize a market. A loss of confidence can trigger a recession. A shift in cultural attitudes toward savings, debt, or consumption can alter economic trajectories for generations. This fragility is not a flaw of the system—it is inherent in any structure built on collective imagination.

Yet this reliance on belief is also a source of resilience. Just as markets can collapse when trust disappears, they can recover when trust is restored. Societies can reinvent currencies, rebuild financial structures, and redefine value according to new moral and cultural needs. The imagination that creates economic instability is the same imagination that enables renewal.

In the end, money is one of humanity's most profound collaborative creations. It is a testament to our ability to build complex systems from intangible foundations. Faith, value, and imagination are not abstract philosophical concepts—they are the invisible architecture holding the global economy together. To understand money is to understand human nature itself: our fears, our hopes, our need for meaning, and our capacity to transform belief into reality.

Sacred Economies of the Ancient World

Long before markets, banks, or digital currencies existed, the earliest human civilizations built economies around sacred principles. Their systems of exchange were not merely practical arrangements for distributing goods; they were expressions of cosmology, ritual, and collective identity. In these ancient worlds, economic life was inseparable from spiritual life. Every transaction, every offering, every measure of grain carried symbolic meaning. To understand these sacred economies is to see how deeply human societies once wove spirituality into material existence—and how traces of that heritage survive in modern financial behavior.

One of the earliest examples comes from Mesopotamia, where temple complexes functioned as economic, religious, and administrative centers. These temples were not simply houses of worship; they were repositories of grain, livestock, and precious materials. Priests oversaw storage, distribution, and record-keeping, interpreting economic order as an extension of divine order. Offerings made by farmers or merchants were both spiritual gifts and contributions to communal welfare. The gods were believed to maintain cosmic balance, and human stewardship of resources mirrored that responsibility. Value flowed through the temple system, reinforcing the idea that prosperity came from alignment with divine will.

In ancient Egypt, the economy revolved around the concept of *maat*—a principle of harmony, justice, and cosmic balance. Wealth distribution, agricultural cycles, and labor obligations were understood through this spiritual framework. The annual flooding of the Nile was interpreted as a blessing from the gods, and in turn, successful harvests were treated as evidence of moral and cosmic alignment. Taxation was not portrayed merely as a civic duty but as a ritual act that renewed the relationship between people, the state, and the divine. When economic disruptions occurred—such as poor harvests or administrative failures—they were seen as fractures in cosmic harmony rather than simple technical problems.

Farther east, ancient China rooted its economic practices in philosophical and spiritual traditions. Under early dynasties, the emperor served as the intermediary between heaven and earth. The Mandate of Heaven conferred legitimacy not only in political matters but also in matters of resource distribution and agricultural regulation. When crops failed or prices inflated, these disturbances were interpreted as signs that the cosmic order had been disturbed—often prompting reforms, rituals, or changes in leadership. The economy, in this worldview, was not a neutral mechanism but a living reflection of moral and spiritual integrity.

Indigenous societies across the Americas also developed sacred economies grounded in reciprocity rather than accumulation. Among many tribes, wealth was measured not by how much one kept but by how much one gave. Ceremonies like the potlatch in the Pacific Northwest functioned as both economic redistribution and spiritual expression. Feasting, gifting, and the destruction of valuables symbolized the cyclical nature of abundance and the belief that hoarding disrupted spiritual balance. In these cultures, economic activity reinforced social bonds and honored ancestral guidance. The sacred and the material were woven into a single fabric of meaning.

In South Asia, the Vedic and later Hindu frameworks infused economic life with spiritual significance. Concepts like *dharma* (duty), *artha* (prosperity), and *karma* shaped views on wealth, work, and ethical conduct. Wealth acquired without righteousness was considered spiritually dangerous, while generosity—*dāna*—was a sacred obligation. Markets thrived, but traders operated under spiritual rules that emphasized fairness and cosmic equilibrium. Commerce existed not in opposition to spirituality but as one expression of it.

Ancient Greece, though often credited with rationalizing economic thought, also viewed wealth through a sacred lens. Temples accumulated treasures, offerings, and financial deposits. The Oracle of Delphi influenced trade routes, colonization decisions, and resource allocation. Even early coinage carried images of gods, linking political and commercial authority directly to divine symbolism. Money itself was treated as an object with spiritual and political resonance, not merely as a tool of exchange.

Across all these societies, one pattern emerges: economic activity required legitimacy, and legitimacy flowed from spiritual frameworks. Trade, taxation, labor, and wealth were justified not through secular logic alone but through narratives of divine order, cosmic balance, ancestral duty, or moral obligation. People trusted their economic systems because they trusted the spiritual stories supporting them.

This is the crucial insight. Sacred economies were not primitive versions of modern markets; they were integrated systems that recognized a truth modern societies often ignore—that value comes from shared meaning, and meaning comes from collective belief. When trade was conducted under the eyes of gods or ancestors, trust was reinforced, and economic cooperation became a spiritual practice.

Even today, echoes of these sacred economies remain. We treat national currencies with reverence, celebrate symbols of prosperity, and respond emotionally to economic rituals such as budgets, interest rate announcements, or market openings. Modern economies appear secular, but they are still shaped by the same human impulse: to root value in something larger than ourselves.

The sacred economies of the ancient world remind us that money has always been more than a material exchange. It has been a reflection of how societies understand purpose, morality, and belonging. In recognizing this heritage, we also recognize that economies collapse not merely from material shortages but from fractures in the shared beliefs that once held them together.

The Moral Weight of Wealth

Wealth has never been a neutral concept. Across cultures and eras, it has carried a moral charge—sometimes celebrated as a sign of virtue or divine favor, and at other times feared as a source of corruption, imbalance, or spiritual danger. Even in today's secular, data-driven economies, the moral weight of wealth quietly shapes our attitudes, behaviors, and political debates. To understand modern economic life, we must first understand why wealth triggers such deep ethical questions and why societies have always linked material abundance to moral responsibility.

In many ancient traditions, wealth was viewed through the lens of cosmic balance. Too much accumulation by one person or group was believed to disrupt social harmony. The idea was not rooted in envy but in the recognition that resources were finite and interconnected. Hoarding was seen as a spiritual offense because it threatened the well-being of the community. This belief created moral obligations for those who had more: to redistribute, to support the vulnerable, and to ensure that prosperity flowed rather than stagnated. Wealth was a stewardship, not a possession.

Religions around the world formalized these expectations. In Judaism, the concept of *tzedakah* frames charity as justice, not generosity. Christianity warns against the dangers of greed, emphasizing humility and compassion. Islam embeds economic ethics in the practice of *zakat*, turning wealth redistribution into a spiritual duty. Buddhism teaches that attachment to material possessions leads to suffering. Though their doctrines differ, these traditions all treat wealth as something morally consequential—capable of uplifting or corrupting depending on how it is used.

Modern economies claim to be secular spaces governed by efficiency, choice, and market logic. Yet the moral dimension has not disappeared; it has simply changed form. Societies still judge wealth, but now through cultural narratives rather than formal doctrine. Self-made success is often celebrated as evidence of discipline, intelligence, or hard work. Extreme wealth, however, can provoke suspicion, resentment, or moral critique, especially when it appears disconnected from social contribution. Conversely, poverty is sometimes framed not as misfortune but as personal failure, revealing how deeply moral assumptions shape economic narratives.

This moral framing influences political discourse as well. Debates over taxation, welfare, corporate power, and inequality are rarely just technical disagreements—they are arguments about fairness, responsibility, and who deserves what. When nations discuss whether the wealthy should pay more taxes or whether social programs should be expanded, they are engaging in moral reasoning disguised as fiscal policy. Even the language used—"burden," "reward," "handout," "justice"—reveals the ethical weight underlying economic decisions.

On a psychological level, wealth changes how people perceive themselves and how they behave. Studies show that as individuals accumulate more, they often develop a heightened sense of autonomy and entitlement. They may begin to see their success as entirely self-earned, even when structural advantages, timing, or luck played significant roles. This can lead to moral blindness—a diminished awareness of how one's actions affect others. Conversely, those without wealth may internalize shame or inadequacy, even when their struggles stem from systemic barriers rather than personal shortcomings. The moral weight of wealth, therefore, shapes emotional landscapes as much as material ones.

Yet wealth also has the power to inspire profound acts of generosity. Many individuals feel a heightened sense of duty as they become more prosperous, using their resources to support communities, fund innovations, or address social issues. Philanthropy, though sometimes criticized as a substitute for equitable systems, reflects a recognition that wealth carries ethical implications. Even small acts—sharing, gifting, supporting family—demonstrate that humans instinctively connect material abundance with moral obligation.

At a collective level, civilizations are judged by how they distribute their prosperity. When wealth circulates, societies flourish; when it concentrates, they fracture. Economic inequality often precedes political instability, social polarization, and loss of trust in institutions. The moral weight of wealth becomes a structural force, influencing how communities hold together—or fall apart. A society that permits extreme disparities without addressing their moral consequences risks eroding its own foundations.

The danger lies in believing that wealth is either inherently virtuous or inherently corrupt. Both extremes oversimplify the human experience. Wealth does not create moral character; it reveals and amplifies it. Those driven by fear may hoard. Those guided by compassion may share. Those motivated by ambition may innovate. Those shaped by insecurity may cling tightly to what they have. Money becomes a mirror of the inner world, reflecting values back into the fabric of society.

Understanding the moral weight of wealth is essential because it determines how individuals use their resources, how communities distribute opportunity, and how nations envision justice. Wealth is not merely an economic force—it is a moral force, shaping choices, identities, and futures. When societies acknowledge this, they can build economies rooted not only in efficiency but in humanity, balance, and a deeper sense of collective purpose.

Chapter 4
Digital Currency and the New Global Order

The world is moving toward a profound transformation in how value is stored, exchanged, and controlled. What began as a slow shift from coins to paper, and from paper to plastic, has accelerated into a global race to redefine money itself in digital form. This transition is not merely technological; it represents a reconfiguration of economic power, political authority, and individual freedom. As physical cash fades from daily life, the systems that replace it will shape the future of civilization in ways we are only beginning to grasp.

Digital currency is often marketed as a convenience—faster payments, simpler transactions, seamless integration with modern life. But beneath the surface lies a deeper structural shift. When money becomes entirely digital, it becomes programmable, traceable, and subject to new forms of oversight. The institutions that issue and regulate currency gain unprecedented visibility into economic behavior. Governments view digital systems as tools for security, efficiency, and economic stability. Corporations see them as opportunities for data-driven profit and market dominance. Citizens, meanwhile, face a future where their financial autonomy depends on the architecture of digital networks they cannot fully see or control.

At the center of this shift are Central Bank Digital Currencies (CBDCs), poised to become the backbone of tomorrow's financial system. They promise stability, but they also introduce mechanisms of surveillance and control that have no historical precedent. Decisions about how these currencies function—whether transactions can be tracked, limited, taxed, or reversed—will determine how much freedom individuals retain in a cashless world.

This chapter examines the implications of losing physical money, the rise of CBDCs, and the reshaping of economic power in a fully digital civilization. The end of cash is not simply a change in payment methods; it is the beginning of a new global order built on digital architecture and political intent.

The End of Physical Money

For most of human history, money has been something people could hold—metal coins stamped with authority, paper notes carrying the weight of national symbols, or even earlier forms like shells, beads, and carved stones. Physical money offered a reassuring solidity. It could be exchanged hand-to-hand without mediation, preserved in a drawer, hidden under a mattress, or carried across borders. Its presence gave a sense of autonomy: you controlled what you physically possessed. But the modern world is rapidly approaching a point where cash becomes an artifact of the past, replaced by digital forms of value that exist only as data. This transition, while subtle at first glance, carries profound implications for freedom, privacy, and the structure of economic power.

The decline of physical money began quietly with the rise of debit cards, credit systems, and online banking. Each innovation increased convenience, making cash seem cumbersome by comparison. The shift accelerated as e-commerce expanded, mobile payments emerged, and everyday transactions—from bus fares to utility bills—moved into the digital realm. Then the COVID-19 pandemic added a final push, as governments and businesses promoted contactless payments for safety. Many consumers, once hesitant, adapted quickly. For younger generations, physical money already feels antiquated, something occasionally required but rarely preferred.

Yet the decline of cash is not simply a matter of consumer preference. It reflects a deeper reengineering of economic systems. When transactions occur digitally, they pass through institutional gateways—banks, payment processors, digital wallets—that record, analyze, and sometimes monetize every interaction. Physical money once offered anonymity; digital money exposes patterns. Physical money provided resilience during system failures; digital systems depend on uninterrupted infrastructure. The convenience of a cashless society obscures its hidden trade-offs: every transaction leaves a footprint, every purchase becomes a data point.

Governments, too, have incentives to minimize cash. Physical currency enables tax evasion, informal economies, and untraceable exchanges. By reducing cash, states gain greater insight into economic activity and greater ability to enforce compliance. Law enforcement agencies often argue that eliminating cash curtails crime. While partially true, this rationale often masks another reality: digital transactions centralize visibility and control. When all money becomes trackable, privacy becomes conditional—granted by institutions rather than inherent in the medium itself.

Financial institutions similarly benefit. Digital transactions generate fees, data, and dependence. Cash empowers individuals to stay outside the formal financial system; digital money draws them into it. Banks gain both revenue and influence as more people rely on their infrastructure. Large corporations—especially technology and payment platforms—profit from transaction metadata, which fuels targeted advertising, behavioral prediction, and algorithmic modeling. In effect, the end of physical money expands the power of institutions and reduces the autonomy of individuals, even when presented as progress.

For many people, this loss of autonomy will go unnoticed—until disruptions occur. In a fully digital system, outages, cyberattacks, policy changes, or account freezes can instantaneously render someone unable to transact. Natural disasters, political instability, or financial crises may expose the vulnerability of infrastructure-dependent money. When physical cash disappears, so does the fallback option that historically helped societies navigate emergencies. Cash, in its simplicity, functioned as a stabilizer not easily replaced by code.

Culturally, the disappearance of cash alters how people think about value. Physical money has weight, texture, and presence. It creates emotional awareness—handing over a banknote feels different from tapping a card or clicking a button. Digital transactions, by contrast, diminish friction. Spending becomes abstract, almost effortless. This abstraction can reshape financial behavior, increasing impulsivity and weakening the psychological boundaries that once grounded economic decisions. What was once a mindful action becomes a background motion, nearly invisible in daily life.

Yet the end of physical money also opens new possibilities. Digital systems can increase efficiency, reduce corruption, streamline global commerce, and enhance financial inclusion for those previously excluded from formal banking. For many developing nations, mobile payments have already accelerated economic growth. Digital currencies can reduce theft, simplify international transactions, and create opportunities for innovation. The challenge lies not in the technology itself but in the governance, ethics, and power structures that determine how that technology is used.

The real transformation is not the disappearance of coins and notes but the shift in who controls the medium of exchange. When money becomes digital, it becomes programmable—and programmability invites intervention. Future systems may allow authorities to restrict how funds are spent, impose expiration dates on currency, or tailor financial incentives and penalties on an individual basis. These capabilities, while potentially useful for economic management, carry implications that societies have barely begun to confront.

The end of physical money marks a turning point in human history. For thousands of years, wealth could be held in the hand, transferred privately, and protected outside institutional oversight. As we transition into a cashless world, we gain convenience but risk losing forms of freedom once taken for granted. The question now is not whether physical money will disappear—its decline is nearly inevitable—but what kind of society will emerge when all value exists as information, and who will wield authority over that information.

In a world without cash, the architecture of money becomes the architecture of power.

Central Bank Digital Currencies and Control

As physical money recedes, governments around the world are preparing a replacement—not private cryptocurrencies, not commercial bank deposits, but **Central Bank Digital Currencies (CBDCs)**. These state-issued digital forms of national currency promise efficiency, speed, and modernized financial infrastructure. Yet beneath these promises lies a deeper transformation—one that shifts the balance of power between citizens and the state in ways few societies have fully reckoned with. CBDCs represent not merely a new type of money, but a new architecture of control.

Unlike cash, which allows anonymous, peer-to-peer transactions, CBDCs are fully traceable. Every payment, transfer, or saving decision becomes a data entry recorded in real time by the issuing central bank or its designated authorities. This traceability provides governments with unprecedented visibility into economic behavior. Tax evasion, black-market transactions, and illicit financial activity become easier to detect. But with visibility comes the possibility of surveillance—continuous, comprehensive, and unavoidable. A CBDC system can reveal not only how much a person spends, but where, when, and on what. The boundary between economic oversight and personal monitoring grows thin.

Control extends beyond observation. Because CBDCs are programmable, central banks can embed rules directly into the currency. They could restrict where funds can be spent—allowing stimulus money, for instance, to be used only for essentials. They could impose automatic taxes at the point of transaction. They could limit or block purchases deemed harmful, risky, or politically sensitive. While such tools could theoretically support public welfare or stabilize economies, they also risk concentrating immense authority in the hands of central institutions. Monetary policy becomes granular, customizable down to the individual, and potentially coercive.

One of the most discussed capabilities is **expiring money**. A CBDC can be designed with a built-in timer, pushing consumers to spend rather than save during recessions. From an economic perspective, this may stimulate demand. But for individuals, it undermines the fundamental notion of money as a store of value. Savings become conditional. The right to hold wealth without expiration becomes a privilege granted—or revoked—by policymakers.

Governments could also implement **tiered access**. Certain citizens might receive different interest rates, transaction limits, or account features based on income, social behavior, or economic status. A CBDC system can reward compliance or punish deviation by modifying a user's financial capabilities. This granular interventionism has no historical precedent, because no currency has ever been programmable at such a micro level. The potential for abuse does not require authoritarian intent at the outset; it requires only the slow normalization of control during emergencies, crises, or periods of political instability.

Another implication lies in the relationship between central banks and commercial banks. With CBDCs, individuals might hold accounts directly with the central bank, bypassing traditional financial institutions. This could reduce banking costs and improve inclusion, but it also reshapes financial power. In times of crisis, citizens might move money from commercial banks into CBDCs, triggering bank runs in mere seconds. Central banks would need mechanisms to control inflows and outflows, reinforcing their central role in the entire financial system. The more they intervene to maintain stability, the more influence they accumulate over everyday financial life.

The geopolitical stakes of CBDCs are equally significant. Nations that deploy successful digital currencies could reshape global trade and challenge existing monetary hierarchies. The dominance of the US dollar, for instance, may be weakened if other nations create digital alternatives that accelerate cross-border payments. Meanwhile, authoritarian states may use CBDCs to consolidate internal control, linking financial identities to social-credit systems or political compliance. Democracies, too, are not immune; crisis-driven policy shifts can expand state power rapidly and often permanently.

Public debate around CBDCs tends to focus on technical efficiency—faster payments, lower costs, improved financial inclusion. These benefits are real, but they obscure the more profound question: **What happens to civic freedom when every transaction is traceable and every unit of currency programmable?** Cash gave individuals the ability to act privately, to dissent quietly, to support causes without oversight. CBDCs eliminate that space unless explicitly designed with privacy protections that few governments currently prioritize.

The rise of CBDCs marks a turning point. They could usher in equitable, modernized systems—or they could create infrastructures of financial control unlike anything the world has seen. The challenge is not the technology itself, but the intentions, safeguards, and limits society chooses to impose. The future of money will hinge not on algorithms or ledgers, but on the balance between efficiency and liberty, convenience and autonomy.

In a cashless civilization shaped by CBDCs, the question is no longer *how* we use money, but *who controls it—and to what end.*

Economic Power in a Cashless Civilization

When a civilization moves fully into a cashless world, the architecture of economic power undergoes a profound transformation. Physical money once distributed power horizontally: anyone holding cash possessed economic agency independent of institutions. In a digital-only civilization, that informal power shrinks. Control shifts upward—toward governments, central banks, multinational payment platforms, and technological infrastructures that mediate every transaction. The disappearance of cash does not merely modernize payments; it rewires the balance of power across society.

One of the first shifts is **the consolidation of financial gatekeeping**. In a cashless world, every interaction—buying food, paying rent, transferring wages—flows through digital rails. These rails are managed not by individuals but by networks: central banks, major financial institutions, and private payment companies. Whoever controls these networks controls participation in the economy. Access to financial life becomes conditional, governed by rules, algorithms, and policies that may be opaque or inflexible. The capacity to freeze accounts, reverse transactions, or block payments becomes not a theoretical risk but a structural feature. Economic rights depend on digital permissions.

At the same time, **data becomes currency**. Every transaction leaves a trail of behavioral information—what people buy, when they buy, how often, and in what patterns. In a cashless civilization, this information accumulates at unprecedented scale. Corporations use it to predict consumer behavior, optimize pricing, and influence purchasing decisions. Governments rely on it for taxation, security, and regulatory enforcement. Data-driven economic models become more powerful than traditional financial analysis. Those who possess the data—big tech platforms, state agencies, analytics firms—gain leverage that exceeds the influence once held by banks alone.

This shift affects social hierarchy as well. People with strong digital literacy, financial access, and technological integration gain an advantage in navigating the economy. Those without these capabilities risk exclusion. A cashless world reduces informal markets—street vendors, day laborers, rural communities relying on physical exchange. Economic opportunity becomes entwined with technological infrastructure. The "unbanked" are no longer simply underserved; they are marginalized by design. Inclusion requires connectivity, identification, and institutional trust.

In a cashless civilization, **economic vulnerability takes new forms**. Outages, cyberattacks, infrastructure failures, or political instability can freeze entire societies. Without cash as a fallback, resilience weakens. A malfunction in payment networks, a corrupted database, or a widespread power failure could paralyze commerce instantly. The fragility is systemic: efficiency replaces redundancy, but at the cost of robustness. Economic life becomes brittle, dependent on uninterrupted digital continuity.

The power of corporations also expands. Companies operating digital payment systems or financial platforms—tech giants, fintech companies, processors—become quasi-governments. They set terms, fees, and rules that shape global commerce. Their influence crosses borders more easily than national regulations. In a cashless world, corporations no longer simply facilitate transactions; they mediate them, analyze them, and profit from their traceability. This economic intermediation becomes a new form of soft power, capable of shaping consumer habits, access to credit, and even political behavior.

Governments, meanwhile, acquire tools previously unimaginable. Tax collection becomes automated, welfare distribution instantaneous, and oversight comprehensive. Shadow economies shrink, but personal privacy shrinks with them. Financial transparency becomes universal not by choice but by default. Political leaders gain the ability to incentivize or restrict economic behavior with surgical precision—rewarding certain industries, discouraging specific purchases, or penalizing undesirable actions through programmable financial tools. Economic policy becomes more efficient, but also more intrusive.

In international relations, a cashless civilization alters geopolitical power. Countries with advanced digital infrastructures, strong cybersecurity, and globally accepted digital currencies gain strategic advantage. Nations that lag technologically risk isolation. The currency dominance that once depended on military might or natural resources increasingly depends on digital adoption, cross-border payment networks, and global trust in technological systems. Economic influence becomes entangled with cyber capability and financial surveillance.

The cultural meaning of money also changes. Physical cash symbolized independence, privacy, and direct exchange. Digital currency symbolizes integration, efficiency, and oversight. Citizens come to see themselves less as free actors and more as nodes in a managed economic ecosystem. The psychological distance between the individual and the system grows. Money becomes not something one holds, but something one accesses—granted by institutions, governed by algorithms, and monitored continuously.

Still, a cashless civilization also brings opportunities. Financial inclusion can expand through mobile systems. International remittances can become faster and cheaper. Corruption may decline as opaque cash flows shrink. Economic planning becomes more precise. Innovation accelerates. The benefits are real—but they exist alongside real dangers.

Ultimately, the question is not whether civilization will become cashless—it is already happening—but what kind of power structure will define that future. Will digital money empower individuals through transparency and access? Or will it centralize authority to unprecedented degrees? A cashless world is not just a technological evolution; it is a political, social, and moral threshold.

In crossing it, humanity must decide who controls the code behind our currencies—and, by extension, the contours of our freedom.

Chapter 5
Inequality at the Edge of Collapse

Inequality is not simply a numerical imbalance between rich and poor—it is a structural force that shapes the destiny of civilizations. History shows that societies rarely collapse because they run out of resources or face external threats alone. More often, they fall when their internal fabric begins to tear, when the distance between those who have everything and those who struggle for basic stability becomes too vast to sustain social trust. In the modern world, that distance is widening at a pace unmatched in recorded history.

Today, wealth concentrates in the hands of a global ultra-elite whose assets rival the GDP of entire nations. Meanwhile, the middle class—the stabilizing core of democratic and economic life—erodes under rising costs, stagnant wages, and financial insecurity. Below them, a vast majority navigates precarity, juggling debt, housing challenges, and limited opportunities. This stratification is not accidental; it is the result of economic systems designed to reward capital over labor, scale over fairness, and efficiency over human well-being.

The consequences extend far beyond economics. Extreme inequality reshapes culture, politics, mental health, and collective identity. It undermines faith in institutions, fuels polarization, and gives rise to social movements born from frustration and despair. Societies fractured by inequality struggle to respond to crises because cooperation becomes rare and trust evaporates. When people no longer believe the system works for them, stability becomes an illusion.

This chapter examines the rise of the ultra-elite, the shrinking middle class, and the growing desperation of the majority. It explores how extreme wealth gaps corrode social cohesion and push civilizations toward tipping points. Inequality is not just a symptom of collapse—it is one of its most reliable precursors, silently shaping the direction of the future long before the break becomes visible.

The Rise of the Ultra-Elite Class

The emergence of an ultra-elite class—individuals whose wealth eclipses not just their fellow citizens but entire nations—marks one of the most significant structural transformations in modern history. Although inequality has existed in every civilization, the scale, speed, and global coherence of today's wealth concentration are unprecedented. The ultra-elite now shape economic systems, political landscapes, cultural narratives, and technological futures in ways that previous aristocracies could only imagine. Their rise signals not merely a shift in income distribution, but a reconfiguration of societal power itself.

The roots of this phenomenon lie in the architecture of contemporary capitalism. Over recent decades, economies have increasingly rewarded ownership over labor, capital over contribution, and scale over craftsmanship. The individuals who dominate these systems tend to control platforms, technologies, or financial instruments capable of extracting exponential gains. It is not uncommon for a single founder to accumulate more wealth in a year than millions of workers combined. This disproportionate accumulation is made possible by technological leverage—software, automation, global networks—that amplify human output far beyond historical norms. What once required thousands of employees can now be achieved by a handful of engineers and an algorithm.

Financial markets further accelerate elite wealth. Stock valuations, venture capital growth, asset inflation, and complex financial instruments concentrate value in the hands of those already positioned at the top. The ultra-elite benefit from compounding advantages: access to exclusive investment opportunities, insider networks, and structural protections that magnify returns while minimizing risk. Wealth becomes not just a resource but a multiplier; once a person crosses a certain threshold, the system begins to work for them automatically.

The political implications are profound. Ultra-elite individuals wield influence through lobbying, campaign financing, think tanks, philanthropy, and media ownership. Their preferences shape policy debates, regulatory environments, and national priorities. While some use their influence to promote social progress, others deploy it to protect self-interest, often resisting reforms that would reduce inequality. When wealth becomes synonymous with political voice, democratic processes tilt toward oligarchy. Citizens may still vote, but the range of viable policy options narrows, filtered through elite consensus long before reaching the public sphere.

Culturally, the ultra-elite occupy a symbolic role that reinforces their dominance. Their lifestyles—visible through media, entertainment, and digital platforms—set aspirational standards that reshape societal values. The myth of meritocracy intertwines with the myth of the billionaire genius, creating narratives that normalize extreme concentration of wealth as evidence of exceptional talent or destiny rather than structural imbalance. These stories obscure the reality that many ultra-elite fortunes emerge not solely from innovation but from system design: tax advantages, monopolistic growth, inherited capital, and global regulatory gaps.

A key feature distinguishing today's ultra-elite from historical aristocracies is their **global mobility**. Wealth is no longer tied to geography. Assets move seamlessly across borders, sheltered in trusts, digital markets, offshore centers, and diversified portfolios. This fluidity allows the ultra-elite to operate above national constraints, selecting jurisdictions that maximize benefit and minimize oversight. As a result, their interests can diverge dramatically from those of the nations they profit from, creating tension between globalized wealth and localized citizenship.

Meanwhile, the benefits of economic growth increasingly flow upward. Productivity rises, but wages stagnate. Companies expand, but workers face precarity. Housing, education, and healthcare grow costlier, pushing opportunity further out of reach for ordinary people. As public goods deteriorate, private alternatives flourish—elite schools, elite clinics, elite enclaves—deepening social fragmentation. The ultra-elite build parallel societies insulated from the struggles of the majority. These divisions weaken the shared identity necessary for social stability.

Perhaps the most consequential aspect of the ultra-elite's rise is their expanding role in shaping the future. A small number of individuals now direct the trajectory of artificial intelligence, biotechnology, space exploration, and digital infrastructure. Their decisions—often made without democratic oversight—will influence how billions live, work, and interact. The concentration of future-defining technologies in elite hands raises existential questions: who decides what progress looks like, who benefits from it, and who bears its risks?

The rise of the ultra-elite class is not inherently catastrophic. Some use their platforms for public good, funding research, supporting philanthropy, or advocating reforms. But the structural imbalance they represent is inherently unstable. History shows that civilizations fracture when elites grow detached from the realities of the majority. The danger lies not in wealth itself but in the widening distance—economic, psychological, political—between those who shape society and those who endure it.

As inequality deepens, resentment grows. Trust erodes. Social cohesion weakens. And civilizations that fail to address this imbalance edge closer to collapse. The ultra-elite class may symbolize innovation and prosperity, but they also embody the fault lines defining humanity's precarious future.

The Shrinking Middle and the Desperate Majority

For generations, the middle class served as the stabilizing backbone of modern civilization—a buffer between extreme wealth and deep poverty, a symbol of upward mobility, and a reservoir of social trust. When the middle class thrived, societies experienced resilience, innovation, and steady progress. But over the last several decades, this foundational group has been slowly and steadily eroding. The decline is not dramatic enough to resemble sudden crisis, yet it is unmistakable in its trajectory: wages stagnate, essential costs rise, job security evaporates, and opportunities narrow. As the middle contracts, the majority slides toward economic desperation, reshaping the social landscape in ways that threaten long-term stability.

One of the primary forces driving this erosion is **the decoupling of productivity and wages**. Workers are producing more value than ever before, yet the financial rewards increasingly flow upward. Adjusted for inflation, median incomes in many countries have barely moved for decades, while the costs of housing, healthcare, education, and basic necessities climb relentlessly. Families that once lived comfortably on a single income now require multiple jobs just to stay afloat. The sense of financial security that defined the middle class has been replaced by constant anxiety—one medical emergency, one job loss, one unexpected bill away from crisis.

The labor market has also shifted toward precarious employment. The rise of contract work, gig platforms, temp jobs, and automation has fractured the traditional pathways to stability. Workers may have employment, but lack benefits, protections, and long-term prospects. Careers that once offered clear progression and retirement security have been replaced by fragmented roles without guarantees. This uncertainty drains psychological resilience. People are forced to think in terms of survival rather than growth, making long-term planning almost impossible.

Education, once considered the reliable ladder to upward mobility, has become both a financial burden and a narrowing gate. Tuition rises far faster than wages, burdening young adults with debt before they even begin their careers. Meanwhile, degrees no longer guarantee stable jobs. The promise that hard work and education lead to prosperity—a foundational belief in many societies—is eroding. When a society's majority no longer trusts its mobility narrative, the emotional fabric weakens, replacing hope with frustration and fatigue.

Housing costs deepen the crisis. In many regions, homeownership—the hallmark of middle-class identity—has slipped out of reach. Housing markets inflated by investment firms, speculation, and limited supply force families into lifelong renting, unstable living arrangements, or geographic displacement. Shelter, a basic necessity, becomes a volatile financial gamble. People who once expected to build equity now face constant insecurity.

As these pressures intensify, the **desperate majority** grows. They are not destitute in the traditional sense; many work full-time, sometimes holding multiple jobs. Their desperation is more subtle but equally corrosive:

financial stress, declining health, reduced opportunities for their children, and a widening gap between effort and reward. They feel the system tightening around them, offering fewer paths upward and many more ways to fall behind. The psychological toll is significant—rising depression, burnout, substance abuse, and loss of faith in institutions.

This desperation fuels political and social volatility. When the middle class feels squeezed and the majority feels abandoned, trust in government, media, and financial institutions collapses. Populist movements gain momentum, promising radical solutions to systemic inequality. Polarization intensifies. Public discourse becomes angrier, more fragmented, more tribal. Societies begin to fracture along economic, cultural, and ideological lines. Stability—the defining feature of a strong middle class—gives way to uncertainty and conflict.

Meanwhile, the wealthy retreat into parallel worlds—private schools, private healthcare, secured neighborhoods—further deepening the divide. As the middle shrinks, fewer people share common experiences, and shared identity dissolves. When the majority becomes desperate and the elite become insulated, social cohesion decays. Civilians no longer see themselves as part of a unified whole, but as competitors for dwindling opportunities.

The shrinking middle and expanding desperate majority echo warning signs from history. Civilizations that lose their middle class lose their equilibrium. Without a broad base of economically stable citizens, societies drift toward oligarchy, unrest, or collapse. The decline is not simply economic; it is moral, psychological, and political. A society where the majority lives in chronic stress cannot sustain democratic norms or long-term prosperity.

Reversing this trajectory requires more than economic adjustment; it demands reimagining the social contract. Without intervention, the desperate majority will continue to grow, pushing modern civilization closer to instability. The fate of the middle class is not merely a financial story—it is a reflection of whether societies can still promise a future worth striving for.

Social Erosion in the Age of Extreme Wealth Gaps

Extreme wealth gaps do not simply distort economic charts—they alter the emotional, cultural, and psychological landscape of entire societies. When the distance between the ultra-rich and the majority becomes too wide, the social fabric begins to weaken. Trust erodes. Shared identity fractures. Everyday interactions carry an undertone of resentment or alienation. What emerges is not just inequality, but social erosion—slow, pervasive, and deeply destabilizing.

At the core of this erosion is **the collapse of shared experience**. In a healthy society, people of different classes still interact in common spaces: public schools, public parks, local markets, community institutions. These encounters, though subtle, cultivate empathy and social cohesion. But as wealth gaps widen, the wealthy withdraw into insulated worlds—private schools, private healthcare, gated communities, exclusive clubs, and curated social networks. Their realities drift so far from the everyday struggles of ordinary citizens that mutual understanding becomes nearly impossible. The rich perceive social problems as distant abstractions; the poor see the wealthy as unreachable and indifferent. This psychological distance becomes a political and cultural gulf.

Extreme inequality also **intensifies social comparison**, a powerful driver of insecurity and dissatisfaction. People measure their well-being not only by what they have, but by how they stand relative to others. When the top becomes hyper-visible—through media, celebrity culture, and digital platforms—it magnifies feelings of inadequacy for those below. The result is a pervasive sense of falling behind, even among people who are objectively stable. Emotional exhaustion grows as individuals chase an ideal of success defined by a minority whose resources far exceed those of the average citizen.

As wealth concentrates, **public institutions deteriorate**. Schools, hospitals, transportation systems, and social services rely on broad-based investment. But when elites opt out of public systems, their political motivation to fund them diminishes. They prefer private alternatives, leaving public infrastructure underfunded and overcrowded. This accelerates social erosion by creating a two-tiered reality: one world where services function smoothly, another where they crumble. Those in the lower tier feel abandoned and angry. Those in the upper tier perceive public decline as proof of inefficiency rather than the predictable consequence of withdrawal.

Political polarization thrives in this environment. Inequality deepens suspicion toward leaders, institutions, and even fellow citizens. People begin to vote not for long-term solutions but for immediate emotional relief—anger, rebellion, or revenge against the perceived beneficiaries of a rigged system. Populist movements exploit these fractures by framing society as a battle between "the people" and "the elites," further weakening democratic norms. When citizens lose faith in the legitimacy of the system, compromise becomes impossible and governance gridlocks. The resulting instability feeds back into economic uncertainty, pushing the society closer to crisis.

The erosion extends into the cultural sphere as well. Communities once united by shared narratives—national identity, collective purpose, moral values—become fragmented. Inequality disrupts the sense that "we are in this together." Instead, people inhabit different cultural ecosystems shaped by their economic realities. The wealthy embrace narratives of meritocracy and individualism; the struggling majority leans toward narratives of injustice and betrayal. Art, media, and public discourse reflect this divergence, reinforcing social separation rather than healing it.

Family life also absorbs the strain. Economic insecurity pressures households, leading to higher rates of stress, conflict, and mental health challenges. Parents may work multiple jobs, leaving less time for children. Young adults delay marriage, homeownership, and parenthood because of financial instability. These shifts weaken intergenerational continuity and reduce the sense of belonging that stabilizes societies. When individuals feel unanchored from both community and family, social erosion accelerates.

One of the most dangerous consequences is **the normalization of despair**. When people believe the system no longer offers a meaningful future, motivation shrinks. Civic engagement declines. Creativity diminishes. Violence and crime may rise as individuals resort to survival strategies outside legal frameworks. Inequality does not merely create economic gaps—it reshapes the moral boundaries of society. Behaviors once seen as unacceptable become rationalized when survival is at stake.

In the long arc of history, extreme inequality has been a precursor to unrest, revolution, and civilizational collapse. Social erosion does not happen overnight; it accumulates gradually until the bonds that once held society together become too thin to withstand pressure. Whether through political upheaval, economic breakdown, or cultural fragmentation, civilizations eventually confront the consequences of neglecting social cohesion.

The age of extreme wealth gaps forces modern societies to confront an uncomfortable truth: stability depends not on the prosperity of the few, but on the well-being of the many. Without deliberate action to rebuild trust, strengthen institutions, and restore shared opportunity, social erosion will continue—quietly, steadily—until the society that once felt secure becomes vulnerable to forces it can no longer control.

Chapter 6
Technology, Automation, and the Death of Work

Technology has always reshaped the nature of work, but the current wave of automation, artificial intelligence, and digital transformation represents something far more profound than previous industrial shifts. We are entering an era in which machines do not merely assist human labor—they replace vast segments of it. Tasks that once required creativity, judgment, or emotional sensitivity are increasingly handled by algorithms, robotics, and autonomous systems. This transition is not just economic; it strikes at the emotional and existential core of what work has historically provided: meaning, identity, structure, and purpose.

For centuries, societies have defined individuals through their occupations. Work connected people to community, anchored their sense of contribution, and offered a pathway to security. As technology accelerates, these foundations are beginning to erode. Entire industries face disruption, while new forms of employment fail to absorb displaced workers at the same pace. The promise that innovation creates more jobs than it destroys is no longer guaranteed. Instead, we confront a future where unemployment, underemployment, and precarious labor become chronic features rather than temporary transitions.

This chapter examines three interconnected dimensions of this transformation. First, it explores what happens when machines begin to outperform humans not only in efficiency but in emotional and cognitive tasks, challenging the meaning of human purpose. Second, it investigates the social impact of permanent job disruption—how families, communities, and psychological well-being are reshaped when stable work disappears. Third, it considers the emergence of a new aristocracy: the small group of individuals and corporations who control data, algorithms, and automated infrastructures, accumulating unprecedented power in the process.

The death of traditional work is not merely an economic shift. It is a civilizational turning point—one that forces humanity to reconsider what it means to live, contribute, and find meaning in a world where machines increasingly do the work once reserved for us.

When Machines Replace Human Purpose

The defining characteristic of modern technological progress is not simply that machines can perform tasks faster or cheaper than humans—it is that they can increasingly perform tasks once believed to require the uniquely human qualities of creativity, intuition, emotional intelligence, and judgment. This shift marks a profound rupture in the relationship between work and identity. Throughout history, human purpose has been intertwined with labor. People defined themselves by what they made, what they built, and what they contributed. Work structured daily life, anchored social roles, and provided a bridge between individual effort and collective meaning. When machines begin replacing not only physical labor but the very functions that once defined human worth, societies encounter an existential crisis.

The first stage of this crisis arises invisibly. Automation begins with routine tasks: manufacturing lines, warehouse sorting, transportation logistics. At this stage, machines merely assist or accelerate human labor. But as artificial intelligence matures, it moves deeper into territories humans assumed were exclusively theirs—language, decision-making, pattern recognition, and even creativity. Algorithms write articles, compose music, diagnose illnesses, draft legal documents, drive vehicles, and teach students. Each advancement subtly dislodges a piece of human identity. Work once viewed as skilled becomes automated. Occupations once considered safe from technological disruption suddenly appear vulnerable.

As this replacement accelerates, a psychological void emerges. Humans are not biologically wired to be idle. Purpose is not a luxury; it is a need. For centuries, work has served as a social compass—telling people who they are, what they contribute, and where they belong. When machines assume these roles, individuals confront uncomfortable questions: *If a machine can do my job better than I can, what is the value of my contribution? If society no longer needs my labor, does it still need me?* The erosion of work becomes the erosion of self.

Communities feel this disruption collectively. Workplaces have long been centers of relationships, mentorship, and shared identity. The disappearance of work is not only economic; it is social. When factories close or offices downsize, communities lose more than income. They lose cohesion. People no longer gather daily with shared purpose. The rituals of teamwork, learning, and problem-solving diminish. Loneliness spikes. Mental health deteriorates. Addiction, suicide, and despair rise, not because people lack material resources but because they lack meaning. Automation removes tasks, but it also removes the human bonds built around those tasks.

Another profound consequence emerges: the redefinition of excellence. In an automated world, machines outperform humans in areas once celebrated as marks of intelligence—calculation, memory, speed, precision, and even strategic reasoning. Human strengths that remain—empathy, creativity, moral reasoning—are undervalued in economic systems designed to reward efficiency. Society struggles to redefine what it means to be skilled when machines surpass humans in measurable output. This mismatch deepens the sense of purposelessness. Humans feel obsolete not because they lack talent, but because the system no longer rewards the talents they possess.

Ironically, the more sophisticated machines become, the more humans are pressured to behave like them—efficient, tireless, error-free. Metrics replace mentorship. Productivity replaces craftsmanship. Workers become extensions of algorithms rather than autonomous contributors. In trying to compete with machines, people sacrifice the qualities that make them human. Yet the competition is unwinnable; machines will always be faster, cheaper, and more scalable. The result is a cultural crisis: we elevate values that dehumanize us while diminishing those that enrich us.

The spiritual dimension of this crisis is equally significant. For centuries, religious and philosophical traditions linked human purpose to work—seeing labor as discipline, contribution, or even divine duty. Automation disrupts this alignment. If work no longer anchors identity, where does purpose come from? Some look to creativity, others to relationships, others to self-expression or service. But societies built around work struggle to adapt. Educational systems, political structures, and economic models all assume that work is central. When machines replace human labor, the entire civilizational framework must evolve.

Yet this transformation also carries possibilities. When machines handle the burdens of labor, humans have the opportunity to redefine purpose beyond productivity. Creativity, compassion, learning, and community could become the new measures of contribution. The challenge lies not in the disappearance of work, but in the absence of alternative narratives that give life meaning. Without intentional redesign, societies risk drifting into a future where material abundance coexists with emotional emptiness.

The rise of machines does not destroy human purpose—it forces a profound re-examination of it. Whether this becomes a crisis or a renaissance depends on whether societies can imagine new forms of meaning that transcend the traditional link between labor and identity. The question is not whether machines will replace human tasks; they already are. The question is whether humanity can rediscover purpose in a world where work is no longer the defining measure of human worth.

The Social Impact of Permanent Job Disruption

Permanent job disruption is not merely an economic trend—it is a profound social transformation that reshapes the very architecture of everyday life. When technological change accelerates beyond society's ability to adapt, work is no longer a temporary challenge but a chronic condition. Generations grow up expecting instability, and a culture once anchored in professional identity begins to fracture. The disruption becomes a background hum that defines how families plan, how communities function, and how individuals imagine their futures.

One of the first and most visible consequences is psychological. Losing a job has always been stressful, but when job loss becomes widespread and structural, it creates a collective sense of insecurity. People no longer fear losing a single job; they fear losing the *idea* of stable employment altogether. Anxiety becomes a societal baseline. Individuals question their relevance, their capacity to adapt, and their long-term prospects.

Even those who remain employed feel the pressure—knowing that their roles, too, could evaporate with the next algorithmic breakthrough or corporate restructuring. Under such conditions, mental health issues rise: depression fueled by uncertainty, burnout from constant skill-chasing, and a pervasive sense of exhaustion rooted not in hard work, but in perpetual adaptation.

Families also absorb the shock. The traditional rhythm of family life—built around working hours, weekends, and predictable routines—slowly dissolves when work becomes unstable. Parents face new pressures as they navigate gig jobs, irregular shifts, or long periods of unemployment. Children observe the stress and internalize it, growing up with a sense that adulthood offers fewer guarantees than it once did. Long-term financial plans become nearly impossible. Saving for college, purchasing a home, or planning for retirement becomes a gamble rather than a reliable trajectory. The future feels negotiable in the worst way: not a promise, but a moving target.

Communities experience an even deeper rupture. Workplaces have long served as social ecosystems—spaces where people meet friends, build networks, and share a sense of belonging. When industries decline or jobs vanish, these ecosystems collapse. Towns built around factories, mines, or regional industries wither into landscapes of abandoned stores, hollowed-out neighborhoods, and strained local services. Schools lose funding as families relocate or income levels fall. Small businesses struggle as purchasing power declines. Social bonds weaken because the common spaces that once connected neighbors disappear. In such environments, isolation grows, and trust recedes.

This erosion of community structure often fuels political volatility. When people feel economically abandoned, they search for explanations—and for those who promise solutions. Populism thrives in the cracks created by job disruption. Narratives of blame, resentment, and scapegoating become persuasive because they offer emotional clarity in a world that feels unpredictable. Groups fracture along ideological, racial, or generational lines as each searches for someone to fault. Economic insecurity, when widespread, becomes a gateway to social polarization.

Another consequence is the rise of a new social hierarchy. As stable employment becomes scarce, society begins categorizing people not by class or profession, but by *adaptability*. Those with access to education, digital tools, and flexible skill sets thrive in the new economic order. They navigate automation by constantly reskilling, pivoting careers, or leveraging digital platforms. Meanwhile, those without these advantages fall further behind. The gap widens not just in income, but in cultural worldview. A stratification emerges: the permanently adaptable versus the permanently displaced. This divide is harder to bridge than traditional class lines because it is psychological as much as economic.

Permanent job disruption also transforms political expectations. Citizens once viewed governments as guarantors of opportunity. In a disrupted economy, they increasingly expect protection—unemployment benefits, retraining programs, universal basic income, or stronger safety nets. Yet governments often move slower than technology, leaving millions in limbo. The mismatch between technological speed and policy inertia creates frustration on both sides. Citizens feel abandoned; institutions feel overwhelmed. As trust erodes, democratic participation declines, and civic apathy expands.

Culturally, the meaning of success shifts dramatically. In past generations, success was associated with career longevity, professional mastery, and upward mobility. Now, success is tied to resilience, improvisation, and the ability to navigate instability. While these traits are valuable, they place immense pressure on individuals to constantly reinvent themselves. This perpetual self-optimization becomes a source of stress, not empowerment. A society that never pauses is a society that struggles to breathe.

Yet within this disruption lies a paradoxical opportunity. With traditional work weakened, new forms of community and purpose can emerge—based on creativity, volunteering, shared projects, or cooperative ventures. But these alternatives require intentional cultivation. Without conscious social design, society risks drifting into fragmentation and despair.

The social impact of permanent job disruption is not simply about employment—it is about the reconfiguration of identity, community, and meaning. If left unmanaged, it can hollow out the foundations of social cohesion. If acknowledged and addressed, it could become the catalyst for a new understanding of purpose and human connection in an era beyond traditional work.

The New Aristocracy of Data and Algorithms

A new ruling class is emerging—one not defined by land ownership, royal lineage, or industrial empires, but by control over data and the algorithms that govern modern life. In earlier eras, elites derived power from physical resources: gold, oil, territory, and labor. Today, the most valuable resource is information, and those who command it shape economies, influence governments, and quietly alter the behavior of billions. This new aristocracy is subtle, largely invisible, and far more powerful than many realize because it operates in realms the average person cannot see, let alone understand.

Data is not simply a collection of facts; it is a map of human behavior. Every message, purchase, search, and click becomes part of a growing archive of human patterns. Those who possess this archive can predict what people will do, influence what they want, and nudge them toward choices that align with institutional or corporate objectives. The modern elite does not need armies or borders. It governs through algorithms—digital systems that decide what people see, how they work, what they buy, and increasingly, what they believe.

The algorithm is the crown of this new hierarchy. It translates raw data into actionable power. Unlike traditional laws or policies, algorithms operate automatically, silently, and at scale. They can influence millions of people simultaneously without appearing coercive. A change in a social media ranking system can reshape cultural norms. An adjustment in credit-scoring algorithms can determine who gets a home or who remains locked out of financial stability. A small tweak in an employment-screening model can erase entire categories of workers from the hiring process.

What makes this aristocracy unique is the asymmetry of understanding. The average person does not know how algorithms function, what data they collect, or why they make certain decisions. Even experts can struggle to explain the inner workings of advanced AI systems. This opacity grants enormous power to the few who design, own, or oversee these systems. Their decisions—often made behind closed doors—carry consequences that ripple through society with extraordinary force. A miscalibrated model can crash markets. A biased dataset can reinforce inequality. A flawed predictive system can criminalize the innocent or overlook the dangerous.

Economically, the data elite consolidates wealth faster than any group in history. Their platforms scale globally with minimal physical infrastructure. Algorithms do not tire, unionize, or demand benefits. As automation expands, data-driven companies gain disproportionate control over productivity and profit. They shape entire industries, from media and retail to healthcare and transportation. While traditional businesses rely on human labor, the new aristocracy relies on computational dominance. This creates a stark divide: those who control the digital infrastructure accumulate exponential wealth, while those outside the system face declining economic relevance.

Culturally, this aristocracy shapes identity and perception. Algorithms determine which voices are amplified and which are buried, whose stories become popular and whose disappear. They create feedback loops that define aesthetics, humor, politics, and even moral frameworks. In earlier centuries, culture was shaped by religious institutions or intellectual elites. Today, it is shaped by recommendation engines and engagement metrics. This shift blurs the line between personal choice and engineered preference. People believe they are choosing freely, yet their choices are often pre-selected by systems optimized for attention, profit, or political alignment.

Politically, the implications are profound. Governments increasingly depend on data-rich corporations for intelligence, infrastructure, and public services. Surveillance systems rely on private algorithms. National security intersects with corporate cybersecurity. Policy decisions are driven by datasets curated by tech giants. In some regions, governments themselves become the data aristocracy—using digital monitoring to exert social control, track dissent, and engineer compliance. The boundary between governance and corporate power grows thinner every year.

Yet the most unsettling aspect of this new aristocracy is its potential permanence. Traditional elites could be overthrown, outvoted, or disrupted by economic change. But data accumulates continuously, and algorithms learn autonomously. Once a company or institution achieves dominance, it becomes nearly impossible to dethrone. The resource they control—the digital behavior of billions—is self-renewing. Even when people are offline, the system continues to learn and predict.

Still, the rise of this new aristocracy does not guarantee a dystopian future. It reveals a crossroads. Societies can demand transparency, establish ethical boundaries, and design systems that distribute power more evenly. But doing so requires a collective awakening—a recognition that data governance is not merely a technical issue but a fundamental question of human freedom.

The aristocracy of data and algorithms is not just a technological phenomenon—it is a reconfiguration of power itself. Whether this becomes a new age of empowerment or a digital feudalism depends on how humanity responds to the forces silently shaping its future.

Chapter 7
Religion, Prophecy, and Economic Fear

Across history, moments of economic uncertainty have always stirred spiritual anxieties. When systems wobble, currencies weaken, or empires lose their footing, people instinctively turn to the stories, symbols, and prophecies that helped earlier generations make sense of chaos. Religion has never been separate from economic life; the two have long shaped one another. Faith traditions offer narratives about justice, suffering, renewal, and ultimate destiny—narratives that become especially powerful when people feel the ground shifting beneath them.

In modern times, financial crises trigger a reaction far deeper than fear of material loss. Markets crash, but so do assumptions about stability, fairness, and control. People search for explanations that go beyond spreadsheets and policy failures. They look for moral meaning in economic events, interpreting them through scriptures, prophecy, or ancient warnings. This instinct is not irrational; it is human. When familiar structures crack, individuals retreat to frameworks that promise coherence, even if those frameworks interpret events in metaphysical terms.

This chapter explores how faith traditions interpret crisis, why apocalyptic narratives gain traction during financial upheaval, and how people seek meaning when economic systems begin to fracture. It examines the psychological function of prophecy—how it stabilizes fear, offers order in chaos, and provides emotional shelter when the future becomes difficult to trust. It also considers how religious and secular apocalyptic thinking subtly influences market behavior, political rhetoric, and collective decision-making.

As economies grow more complex and fragile, these spiritual undercurrents become even more relevant. Economic fear rarely remains economic; it spills into morality, identity, and existential belief.

Understanding this intersection helps us see not just how people react to crisis, but why societies behave the way they do when confronting uncertainty.

How Faith Traditions Interpret Crisis

Across cultures and millennia, religious traditions have served as humanity's earliest analytical frameworks for understanding crisis. Long before economics became a formal discipline, faith communities developed narratives, rituals, and symbolic systems that helped people interpret scarcity, upheaval, and collapse. These interpretations were not merely spiritual; they shaped political choices, social cohesion, and economic behavior. Even in modern, secular societies, the echoes of these ancient interpretive patterns continue to influence how people respond to instability.

Faith traditions begin by framing crisis within a larger story. In many religions, hardship is not random but part of a moral or cosmic sequence. Crisis may signal divine displeasure, a collective moral failure, or a moment of necessary purification. These interpretations transform uncertainty into coherence. Suffering becomes meaningful rather than chaotic, giving individuals a sense of emotional order even when material order collapses. This psychological reframing is powerful. It stabilizes communities by providing shared explanations and shared responsibilities.

In monotheistic traditions, crisis often appears as a form of testing or revelation. Hardship becomes a crucible through which character is refined and communities are urged to return to foundational principles. Economic decline may be interpreted as a reminder to live ethically, share resources, or abandon corruption. Faith communities often respond with renewed solidarity—food drives, mutual caregiving, and charitable systems that fill gaps left by weakened institutions. These actions reinforce the belief that moral conduct, rather than economic randomness, determines outcomes.

Other traditions view crisis cyclically rather than morally. Hindu and Buddhist cosmologies, for example, interpret disruption through cycles of decay and renewal. An economic crash is not necessarily punishment but part of a broader rhythm in which civilizations rise, decline, and eventually regenerate. This worldview encourages resilience by accepting impermanence as natural. Instead of waiting for divine intervention, adherents may focus on internal transformation, ethical living, or spiritual detachment. In such frameworks, the proper response to crisis is not fear but understanding: a recognition that no system—economic or otherwise—is meant to last forever.

Indigenous traditions often interpret crisis through the lens of disrupted balance. Economic collapse may be seen as a consequence of environmental exploitation, broken relationships, or disrespect toward ancestral wisdom. These interpretations highlight interconnectedness rather than moral failure or cosmic cycles. The community's task is to restore harmony—between people, nature, and the spiritual world. This worldview resonates strongly in modern climate-related economic crises, where environmental mismanagement visibly destabilizes markets and livelihoods.

Even secular societies unconsciously mirror these patterns. When stock markets crash or inflation surges, public narratives often take on moral or quasi-religious tones. Commentators speak of "reckoning," "cleansing," or "the consequences of greed." Politicians describe crises as tests of national character or warnings about collective misalignment. These are not purely economic analyses; they are inherited interpretive habits, shaped by centuries of religious storytelling.

During major crises, prophecy also returns to the center of public consciousness. Faith traditions often contain apocalyptic warnings—visions of societal breakdown that resonate powerfully when modern systems falter. Economic panic activates these narratives, giving people a way to articulate fears they cannot fully explain. Prophecy offers structure to the unknown, a roadmap—even if grim—for what might come next. In some communities, economic decline is interpreted as the prelude to a long-foretold transformation. In others, it is a sign that humanity has violated moral or spiritual laws. Regardless of the specific narrative, prophecy becomes a form of cognitive anchoring, helping individuals navigate fear by imagining crisis within a larger destiny.

Yet faith-based interpretations of crisis are not only retrospective; they shape behavior. When communities view downturns as divine tests, they often become more generous. When they interpret crisis as punishment, they may grow stricter or more judgmental. When they view collapse as cyclical, they may practice patience rather than panic. When they see imbalance, they may advocate for ecological or social reform. These interpretations influence how people spend, save, vote, and invest. They affect risk appetite, community engagement, and even the willingness to accept governmental intervention. Financial markets, though driven by numbers, are deeply human. They respond to fear, hope, and imagination—forces shaped profoundly by religious memory.

In the end, faith traditions interpret crisis not merely as economic disruption but as existential commentary. They offer meaning where data falls short and provide frameworks that allow individuals to endure uncertainty without falling into despair. They remind societies that crisis, however severe, is never only material; it is always emotional, psychological, and spiritual. Understanding these interpretive patterns helps us see why economic fear can never be fully separated from the narratives that have guided humanity since its earliest days.

Apocalyptic Narratives and Market Psychology

Apocalyptic narratives—stories of final judgment, cosmic upheaval, and civilizational collapse—have existed for thousands of years. They were shaped in eras of famine, war, and uncertainty, but they continue to influence modern societies in ways that extend far beyond religion. When economies begin to tremble, these narratives resurface with startling intensity. They do not simply fill spiritual space; they shape economic behavior, investment decisions, political reactions, and the psychology of entire populations. Modern financial systems may rely on data, algorithms, and quantitative models, but beneath the surface they operate through emotion, imagination, and fear—forces that apocalyptic thinking amplifies.

Economic fear rarely emerges in a vacuum. When markets fall, people instinctively search for explanations. They want narratives that make sense of volatility, narratives that connect disparate events into a coherent story. Apocalyptic frameworks offer precisely that: a way to interpret instability as part of a larger pattern, whether divine, moral, or historical. Even for those who do not hold religious beliefs, apocalyptic metaphors provide a language to express the magnitude of perceived threat. Investors speak of "meltdowns," "bloodbaths," and "the end of an era" because these hyperbolic terms mirror the emotional weight of financial uncertainty.

This psychological climate has measurable effects on markets. When individuals believe a collapse is imminent, their behavior shifts from rational calculation to survival instinct. They sell assets prematurely, hoard cash, and withdraw from long-term commitments. Fear becomes contagious, and the market becomes a mirror of collective imagination rather than economic fundamentals. A rumor, a prophecy-like prediction from a popular commentator, or a viral social media post can trigger mass sell-offs. In extreme moments, markets behave less like systems governed by logic and more like crowds fleeing an imagined catastrophe.

Apocalyptic narratives also influence policymakers, though often indirectly. Leaders know that public confidence is as crucial to economic stability as monetary policy. When apocalyptic sentiments rise—whether through religious prophecy, conspiracy theories, or cultural pessimism—governments respond with interventions aimed at restoring psychological assurance. Central banks issue reassuring statements. Politicians frame crises as temporary storms rather than existential threats. Yet these responses often reveal how much power apocalyptic thinking holds; they shape not only public emotion but the strategic behavior of institutions tasked with preventing panic.

Another important dimension lies in how apocalyptic narratives create self-fulfilling prophecies. If enough people believe a major crash is unavoidable, they behave in ways that bring one closer to reality. Markets are highly sensitive to expectation. Belief becomes a market force, one that can override fundamentals. This is why financial bubbles and crashes often mirror the emotional arcs of apocalypse stories: a period of irrational growth ("the last days of prosperity"), warnings that go ignored, and a sudden, catastrophic fall. Narrative cycles and market cycles intertwine.

Religious apocalypticism adds another layer of complexity. For some believers, economic crisis is not merely an event but a sign of divine timing. This interpretation can fuel both resignation and bold action.

Resignation, because individuals may see downturns as inevitable and beyond human control. Bold action, because they may believe crisis demands urgent moral or spiritual preparation. In both cases, economic behavior changes. Spending patterns shift. Investments move toward assets perceived as "safe" in an end-times scenario—gold, land, or commodities. Charitable giving may increase or decrease depending on interpretive emphasis. Communities may stockpile goods, creating artificial shortages that further destabilize markets.

The media amplifies this dynamic. Every downturn is framed in dramatic language; every correction becomes a crisis; every recession is described in catastrophic terms. This reflects not only the need for attention but the human craving for narrative structure. Modern journalism unconsciously borrows from apocalyptic storytelling—using cliffhangers, villains, sudden reversals, and impending doom. These narratives shape public sentiment, which in turn shapes market behavior. Even analysts who pride themselves on objectivity often fall into the gravitational pull of dramatic forecasting, because audiences respond more strongly to stories of collapse than to slow, incremental change.

Yet apocalyptic narratives are not solely destructive. They also reveal deep cultural anxieties about inequality, corruption, environmental decay, and the fragility of modern systems. Their popularity during economic crises signals a collective intuition: that something in the system is unsustainable, that current trajectories are untenable, and that society must confront uncomfortable truths. In this sense, apocalyptic psychology becomes a diagnostic tool—a way for populations to articulate fears that policymakers ignore or dismiss.

The interplay between apocalyptic narratives and market psychology shows that financial systems are never purely technical. They are emotional ecosystems, shaped by imagination as much as by interest rates and corporate earnings. When people fear the end of the world—literally or metaphorically—they behave in ways that reshape markets, politics, and social life. Understanding this interplay is essential for understanding why economies behave irrationally in moments of crisis, and why fears of collapse often say as much about human belief as they do about financial reality.

The Search for Meaning When Systems Break

When economic systems fracture, the rupture is not only financial or political—it is existential. People do not merely lose jobs, savings, or stability; they lose the frameworks that once told them who they were and how the world worked. Economic systems, despite their technical language, function as cultural narratives. They give societies a sense of order, purpose, and predictability. When these systems break, the psychological scaffolding that supported daily life collapses with them, creating a void that individuals instinctively seek to fill with meaning.

In times of stability, people rarely question the deeper purpose of their economic routines. They work, earn, spend, save, and plan because the system promises continuity. But when the system falters—when inflation erodes security, markets crash, institutions fail, or inequality becomes unbearable—individuals are forced into uncomfortable self-examination. They ask not only *How will I survive?* but *Why is this happening?* and *What does it say about the world and my place in it?* These questions reach into territory that economics alone cannot address.

In this void, people turn toward frameworks that feel more human than financial spreadsheets—stories rooted in faith, history, identity, or morality. Some return to traditional religious teachings, finding comfort in the idea that suffering fits within a larger cosmic design. Others adopt secular philosophies or political ideologies, reframing collapse as evidence of systemic injustice or as the prelude to necessary transformation. Still others embrace new spiritual movements, conspiracy theories, or esoteric interpretations that offer a sense of control in chaotic times.

This search for meaning is not driven by weakness but by human nature. People are narrative creatures; they cannot endure prolonged uncertainty without crafting explanations that provide emotional coherence. When systems break, meaning becomes a survival tool. It gives individuals the psychological strength to navigate crisis, endure hardship, and imagine a future beyond the immediate wreckage.

Communities also play a crucial role. In periods of collapse, isolation is dangerous. Loneliness magnifies fear, distorts perception, and deepens despair. Collective meaning-making—whether through religious gatherings, political movements, activist groups, mutual aid networks, or even online communities—helps restore a sense of belonging. People come together not only to share resources but to share interpretations. Crisis becomes communal rather than solitary, and meaning becomes a shared creation rather than a private burden.

Interestingly, the search for meaning often reveals truths that remain hidden during prosperity. People begin to question assumptions that once felt unquestionable: the fairness of economic structures, the moral integrity of institutions, the sustainability of consumption-based lifestyles, or the illusion of endless growth. Crisis exposes contradictions that stability conceals. It forces a confrontation with reality, a reckoning with the limits of systems built on fragile foundations. In this sense, meaning is not merely consolation—it is awakening.

Yet this search can take darker turns as well. When systems break and trust erodes, some people gravitate toward explanations that provide a clear enemy or a simple cause. These narratives—whether political extremism, apocalyptic cults, or scapegoating ideologies—offer certainty at the cost of truth. They appeal to individuals who feel powerless, because they transform chaos into a battle with identifiable villains. These narratives can fracture societies further, fueling conflict and deepening division.

Another challenge arises when individuals realize that meaning must be rebuilt, not inherited. Economic systems provide identity through roles—worker, consumer, provider, investor. When those roles collapse, people must redefine themselves. Some find purpose in creativity, caregiving, learning, or community service. Others struggle to replace the lost identity, drifting without direction. The emotional toll is heavy. Grief for a lost system can feel like grief for a lost self.

Despite these difficulties, the search for meaning during systemic breakdown also contains profound possibility. It opens space for reimagining values, priorities, and relationships. People begin to ask what truly matters—security, connection, justice, spirituality, simplicity, dignity—and whether the previous system ever genuinely supported those ideals. Crisis, painful as it is, becomes an opportunity to rebuild meaning on foundations that are more authentic and more resilient.

Ultimately, when systems break, the search for meaning is not a distraction from economic reality—it is a necessary complement to it. Societies cannot rebuild institutions or economies without first rebuilding the narratives that give those systems legitimacy and purpose. Meaning is the invisible architecture that holds civilization together. When it fractures, everything else follows. When it is restored, even in new forms, the path forward becomes visible again.

CHAPTER 8
RESOURCE WARS AND THE ECONOMICS OF SCARCITY

Scarcity has always shaped human history, but in the twenty-first century it is evolving from a background pressure into a defining global force. As populations rise, ecosystems strain, and climate patterns shift, the world is entering an era where essential resources—water, energy, minerals, arable land—are no longer assumed to be abundant. Instead, they are becoming battlegrounds. Nations, corporations, and communities increasingly recognize that the struggle for control over finite resources will determine political power, economic stability, and even survival itself.

Unlike past eras of conflict driven by ideology or territory, modern tensions emerge from deeper structural limits. Rivers are drying, aquifers are depleting, oil fields are aging, and extreme weather destabilizes energy grids and agricultural systems. These pressures do not simply create shortages; they reshape geopolitics. Nations turn inward, building strategic reserves and weaponizing supply chains. Others expand outward, investing in foreign land, ports, and mines to secure long-term access. Scarcity becomes strategy.

This chapter explores how water and energy—the lifeblood of civilization—are rapidly becoming theaters of conflict. It examines how governments and private actors manipulate scarcity as a tool of leverage, coercion, or dominance. And it investigates the emerging landscape of global competition, where aging empires, rising powers, and fragile states navigate a world in which the old assumptions of endless supply no longer hold.

Resource wars are not solely fought with armies; they unfold through trade restrictions, infrastructure investments, cyberattacks on grids, and diplomatic pressure. Understanding this shift is essential, because the economics of scarcity will influence everything from migration patterns to technological innovation and global alliances. In a depleted world, power belongs not just to those who have resources, but to those who control access, distribution, and the narratives that justify their claims.

Water, Energy, and the New Battlegrounds

Water and energy—two elements so fundamental to civilization that their abundance is often taken for granted—are rapidly becoming the central battlegrounds of the twenty-first century. As the planet warms, populations expand, and industrial demands intensify, control over these resources is shifting from a matter of infrastructure to a matter of power. The struggle is no longer hypothetical or futuristic; it is unfolding in real time across continents. What were once invisible background systems now define geopolitical strategy, economic resilience, and national security.

Water is emerging as the most volatile of these battlegrounds. Unlike oil or minerals, it has no substitute. Human life, agriculture, manufacturing, and energy production depend on it. Yet rivers fade, glaciers retreat, and aquifers deplete faster than they can recharge. Regions such as the Middle East, South Asia, and parts of Africa face acute shortages that threaten food supplies and provoke political tensions. As upstream nations build dams and redirect river flows, downstream countries fear losing access to the lifelines that sustain their populations. Water becomes both a bargaining chip and a pressure point. What appears as a technical disagreement over irrigation or hydropower is often a deeper conflict about sovereignty, survival, and historical grievance.

In urban centers, water scarcity produces subtler but equally destabilizing consequences. Megacities struggle with aging infrastructure, contamination, and unequal access. Water becomes a commodity, then a privilege, then a flashpoint for civil unrest. When taps run dry, societies confront the fragility of their most basic systems. Households begin stockpiling. Local governments impose rationing. Businesses relocate. Economic planning becomes reactive rather than strategic. A shortage that begins as a climate or engineering problem quickly becomes a social and political crisis.

Energy, meanwhile, remains the backbone of industrial civilization. But the traditional energy landscape—dominated by fossil fuels, fixed pipelines, and centralized grids—is undergoing a transformation marked by volatility. Oil, once the primary source of geopolitical power, now competes with renewable energy, rare earth minerals, and advanced storage technologies. Yet this shift does not eliminate conflict; it merely relocates it. Nations that once relied on oil exports face declining influence, while those with access to lithium, cobalt, or solar-rich territory rise in strategic importance. The transition to clean energy, rather than creating global harmony, intensifies competition over new forms of resource dominance.

Energy infrastructure itself becomes a battleground. Pipelines are sabotaged or weaponized as leverage. Cyberattacks target electrical grids, threatening blackouts that paralyze cities and economies. Nations invest heavily in securing energy corridors—maritime routes, ports, and undersea cables that keep global supply chains functioning. Even the push toward renewable systems introduces new vulnerabilities: solar and wind technologies depend on supply chains dominated by a few powerful nations. Thus, green energy does not eliminate dependency; it rearranges it.

Water and energy intersect in ways that amplify tension. Hydropower competes with agricultural needs. Desalination plants depend on vast amounts of energy. Droughts reduce the cooling capacity of power stations. Heat waves spike energy demand while lowering water reserves. Nations caught in these feedback loops confront cascading crises that no single policy can resolve. This intersection creates a new strategic reality: whoever controls both water and energy flows controls the future.

Corporations, too, enter the battleground. Multinational companies purchase water rights, invest in private reservoirs, and develop technologies that give them leverage over governments. Energy giants reshape political landscapes with investment, lobbying, and influence. The privatization of essential resources shifts decision-making from public institutions to profit-driven entities. Citizens become consumers rather than stakeholders in the management of their own survival.

In some regions, competition over water and energy drives migration. As agricultural land becomes barren and energy grids fail during extreme weather, families abandon homes in search of stability. These migrations create new pressures on neighboring countries and fuel nationalist backlash. Societies that once debated economic policy must now confront existential questions of capacity: how many can they support, and at what cost?

Yet scarcity does not only generate conflict. It also sparks innovation. Nations develop advanced desalination systems, decentralized energy networks, and smart irrigation technologies. Communities experiment with collective ownership of water resources or localized renewable systems that reduce vulnerability to global shocks. Innovation, however, rarely unfolds evenly. Wealthier nations adapt faster, widening inequalities and reinforcing global hierarchies.

Ultimately, water and energy are no longer neutral elements of daily life. They are strategic assets, bargaining tools, and symbols of modern fragility. The new battlegrounds are not defined by traditional warfare alone but by supply chains, infrastructure, treaties, climate systems, and the invisible flows that sustain civilization. Control over these flows—who gets what, when, and at what cost—will determine the shape of world power in the decades ahead.

Strategic Scarcity as Political Weaponry

Scarcity has always existed, but the modern world has transformed it into a deliberate instrument of power. What was once the accidental result of drought, depletion, or mismanagement is now increasingly engineered, manipulated, or strategically exploited. Nations, corporations, and political actors have discovered that controlling access to essential resources—water, energy, food, minerals—can achieve what armies and treaties often cannot. Strategic scarcity becomes a form of political weaponry, shaping behavior, influencing alliances, and redefining the balance of power without a single shot being fired.

The core logic behind this weaponization is simple: when a resource is essential, whoever controls its flow controls the choices of others. Scarcity produces dependency, and dependency allows leverage. A nation that relies on another for water cannot easily oppose it in geopolitical disputes. A region reliant on a single supplier for energy becomes vulnerable to coercion. Even domestic populations, when confronted with engineered shortages, can be steered toward political outcomes they would otherwise resist. Scarcity does not merely pressure; it disciplines.

Water is one of the most potent examples of this strategy. Rivers that cross national boundaries become instruments of control when upstream nations build dams or divert flows. Downstream countries face reduced irrigation, weakened agriculture, and social unrest. The upstream state gains bargaining power simply by turning a valve. These actions are rarely declared as political; they are framed as development or modernization projects. But the timing, scale, and persistence of water withholding reveal deeper motives. When water becomes a tool of negotiation, diplomacy transforms into a contest of pressure points rather than principles.

Energy, too, has become a strategic chokehold. Nations rich in oil or natural gas exert influence by manipulating supply, adjusting prices, or selectively distributing access. Energy pipelines become political corridors where every disruption, maintenance delay, or pricing shift carries geopolitical meaning. A temporary suspension of fuel exports can destabilize an economy, undermine public confidence, and pressure governments to alter foreign policy positions. Energy scarcity is thus weaponized not through direct confrontation but through the slow erosion of a nation's resilience.

Strategic scarcity also extends to critical minerals—rare earth elements, lithium, cobalt, and other materials essential for modern technology. Nations controlling these supply chains wield influence over global manufacturing, military capabilities, and technological innovation. By restricting exports or monopolizing refining processes, they can stall competitors, shape international markets, and dictate terms of cooperation. Scarcity becomes a lever that shapes not only economies but the technological future of entire regions.

Domestic political actors also exploit scarcity to consolidate power. By controlling access to food, electricity, or fuel, governments can reward loyalty and punish dissent. In authoritarian regimes, distribution becomes a form of political surveillance: those who comply receive access, while those who resist face shortages. Even in democratic societies, scarcity can be framed as the result of external threats, creating fear that leaders use to justify expanded authority or controversial policies. When scarcity is presented as inevitable, populations become more tolerant of government control.

Corporations, too, participate in the strategic deployment of scarcity. Through monopolistic practices, price manipulation, or restrictive licensing, companies can limit the supply of essential goods—from pharmaceuticals to agricultural seeds—to maximize profit and influence regulatory decisions. When private entities control life-sustaining resources, scarcity becomes intertwined with market power, often leaving governments struggling to protect public interests. The line between economic strategy and political coercion blurs.

Psychologically, scarcity amplifies fear and compliance. When people worry about access to water, fuel, or food, they become more susceptible to political narratives that promise stability, even if those narratives undermine freedom or transparency. Scarcity narrows imagination; it makes long-term thinking difficult and forces individuals into survival mode. Political actors know this. That is why scarcity is often timed, dramatized, or selectively emphasized to shape public sentiment. The manipulation of perception becomes as powerful as the manipulation of supply.

In global diplomacy, strategic scarcity changes the nature of alliances. Nations no longer align purely through ideology or geography but through resource interdependence. Countries rich in essential resources gain disproportionate influence, while resource-poor nations must navigate relationships carefully to avoid destabilizing their own supply chains. This dynamic creates a hierarchy not based on military strength but on the control of lifelines. Power becomes fluid, shifting toward those who manage scarcity effectively.

Yet the weaponization of scarcity carries risks. It can provoke retaliation, spark regional conflicts, or push nations toward desperate measures. It undermines trust in international systems and accelerates global fragmentation. But perhaps the greatest danger is that strategic scarcity becomes normalized—an accepted tool of governance rather than a warning sign of systemic breakdown.

In a world increasingly shaped by limits, the ability to create or relieve scarcity becomes a defining political skill. Strategic scarcity is not merely a tactic; it is a new form of power—subtle, pervasive, and profoundly transformative. Understanding it is essential for understanding the future of global conflict, cooperation, and control.

Competing Powers in a Depleted World

As the planet's resources tighten, the structure of global power is undergoing a dramatic transformation. Nations no longer compete in a world defined by abundance or expansion; they compete within the narrowing margins of a depleted Earth. This shift alters everything—from foreign policy and military strategy to economic alliances and cultural narratives. The question is no longer which nation can grow the fastest, but which can endure the longest under conditions of scarcity. In such an environment, power is measured not only by military strength or economic output but by access, resilience, and the ability to secure essential lifelines in the face of systemic decline.

The first major axis of competition forms between established powers and rising states. Long-dominant nations—such as the United States and European powers—built their influence in an era of plentiful resources. Their infrastructures, political systems, and economic models still assume access to cheap fuel, stable climates, and global trade. But these assumptions weaken as energy supplies tighten, climate volatility disrupts agriculture, and global markets fracture under geopolitical pressure. Established powers face the paradox of needing to maintain influence while adapting to conditions that undermine the foundations of that influence.

Rising powers, especially China and India, confront a different challenge. Their populations are massive, their industrial demands enormous, and their energy needs expanding. They enter an international arena where competition is fiercer and margins tighter. Their strategies revolve around aggressive external investments—ports, mines, farmland, rare-earth facilities—as they seek to secure resource pipelines for the next century. These acquisitions are not expansions of empire in the traditional sense, but extensions of survival: a global network designed to bypass scarcity at home. As these powers grow more assertive, fault lines widen between them and the older powers that once shaped global norms.

Regional powers also emerge as significant actors—not because of economic might but because of geographic advantage. Countries that control river sources, mineral-rich territories, or key transportation corridors become indispensable players. Turkey, Ethiopia, Brazil, and various Central Asian states now influence global dynamics because they sit on essential water routes, fertile land, or rare resource clusters. Their bargaining power increases as scarcity deepens. Larger powers must negotiate, invest, or concede influence to maintain access. Geography becomes destiny once again, but in a world where the strategic value of territory is defined by what it can supply, not how much land it covers.

In this depleted world, alliances shift rapidly. Nations form strategic partnerships based not on ideology but on mutual vulnerabilities. A country rich in hydropower cooperates with one rich in fossil fuels; a nation with advanced desalination technology aligns with one facing severe drought; states with strong food production negotiate exclusive trade deals with those severely affected by climate change. These alliances are often fragile, because scarcity creates conditions where cooperation coexists uneasily with competition. Partners today may become rivals tomorrow if resource pressure intensifies.

Meanwhile, non-state actors gain unprecedented influence. Multinational corporations control critical supply chains—from food distribution to data infrastructure, from pharmaceuticals to rare earth minerals. Their power often rivals that of governments, especially in regions where political instability weakens state capacity. Private companies decide which countries receive essential resources, how supply chains are structured, and who has access to technological innovations. The traditional idea of national sovereignty fractures under the weight of corporate leverage.

Conflict, too, evolves under conditions of scarcity. Wars are no longer fought solely for land or ideology; they target infrastructure, supply routes, and environmental choke points. Cyber warfare becomes a tool to disrupt power grids and water systems. Proxy conflicts emerge around mines, dams, and trade corridors. Nations avoid total war not out of restraint but because complex supply chains make them mutually vulnerable. A global economy built on precarious interdependence becomes an arena where every disruption carries cascading consequences.

Yet despite these tensions, scarcity also pushes nations toward forms of cooperation that did not exist in times of abundance. Climate agreements, water-sharing treaties, and cross-border energy grids emerge from necessity rather than idealism. Powers recognize that certain threats—heat waves, droughts, pandemics, resource collapse—cannot be contained by borders. Cooperation becomes a strategy of self-preservation, not moral conviction.

Still, the overall pattern is clear: in a depleted world, power belongs to those who can secure stability amid uncertainty. This means not only controlling resources but mastering adaptability—technological innovation, resilient infrastructure, diversified supply chains, and strategic diplomacy. The nations that survive and thrive will be those that recognize the new rules of the game early and reshape their systems accordingly.

The struggle among competing powers is not simply geopolitical—it is the story of civilization adapting to its limits. The world that rises from this competition will be defined not by expansion but by endurance.

CHAPTER 9

SURVEILLANCE, CONTROL, AND THE MANAGED CITIZEN

In every era, power adapts to the tools available. In the twenty-first century, the most powerful tool is data—not only the information we willingly share, but the vast streams generated by our movements, habits, fears, desires, and routines. Modern surveillance is no longer the crude act of watching; it is the sophisticated science of predicting and shaping behavior. Governments, corporations, and algorithmic systems now possess insights into human patterns that earlier regimes could only dream of. The result is a new model of citizenship: one that is monitored, managed, and subtly influenced at every step.

This chapter explores the economic logic behind surveillance—how watching people becomes profitable, efficient, and strategically essential. It examines how algorithms, once designed to optimize convenience, have evolved into instruments capable of steering emotions, nudging decisions, and shaping social outcomes. Surveillance is not just a security apparatus; it is a business model, a political tool, and increasingly, a cultural norm.

In this new landscape, privacy becomes less a right than a shrinking commodity. The erosion is quiet, incremental, almost invisible. People trade data for convenience, access, and digital belonging, often unaware that the same systems granting them personalized services are also mapping their vulnerabilities. Power no longer operates through force; it operates through information—anticipating dissent before it forms, influencing choices before they fully crystallize, and creating an environment where compliance feels natural rather than imposed.

This chapter examines these dynamics through three lenses: the economic incentives behind constant surveillance, the mechanisms of behavioral engineering through data-driven systems, and the shifting nature of power in a world where privacy is becoming a historical luxury.

As surveillance becomes woven into the architecture of daily life, the challenge is not simply understanding what is being watched, but recognizing how it reshapes who we become.

The Economics of Watching

Modern surveillance is not driven primarily by security or governance—it is driven by economics. Watching people has become one of the most profitable industries in human history. Every click, gesture, location ping, purchase, and conversation feeds an expanding ecosystem of data extraction in which human life is transformed into a raw material. The economics of watching rests on a simple principle: the more a system knows about you, the more precisely it can influence what you do. And influence is the currency that powers digital empires, political campaigns, and global markets.

The origins of this economic model began innocently enough. Early internet companies collected data to improve user experience—faster searches, personalized recommendations, targeted ads. But as technology evolved, the incentives shifted dramatically. Data became not just a way to improve products but a way to predict and steer human behavior. Platforms realized that knowing *why* a person acts matters more than knowing *what* they do. Predictability is profit. Influence is power.

This is where the surveillance economy diverges from traditional business models. Instead of selling products, companies sell behavioral certainty. Advertisers, political strategists, and corporations pay extraordinary amounts for the ability to shape desires, fears, and decisions at scale. The deeper the data, the more accurate the prediction. The more accurate the prediction, the more valuable the influence. Human beings become portfolios of tendencies—risk levels, emotional responses, buying triggers—sold to the highest bidder.

What makes this system uniquely powerful is that it functions invisibly. People rarely sense they are being monitored because surveillance is embedded in the architecture of daily life. Smartphones track movement. Apps map preferences. Websites record browsing patterns. Wearable devices log heart rates and sleep cycles. Even home appliances collect data. Surveillance is no longer an act of watching; it is an ambient environment where existence itself generates profits. The economics of watching depend on this invisibility. The less consumers notice, the more freely they behave—and the more authentic and valuable their behavioral patterns become.

Governments quickly realized the strategic value of this ecosystem. Instead of building their own surveillance networks, many rely on private companies whose data troves exceed anything intelligence agencies once imagined. The boundary between state power and corporate power erodes as governments purchase, request, or discreetly access private datasets. Surveillance becomes a public-private partnership where both sides benefit: corporations gain influence and protection, while governments gain insights into populations at unprecedented granularity.

A defining feature of this economy is its feedback loop. Data does not simply describe human behavior; it shapes it. Algorithms designed to capture attention push people toward content that intensifies emotional engagement—fear, outrage, desire, tribal belonging. This emotional stimulation generates more clicks, more interactions, and therefore more data. Human psychology becomes both the product and the engine of the system. The economics of watching thrive on stimulation, polarization, and addiction because these states create predictable patterns. Calm, reflective citizens are unpredictable; emotionally aroused users are goldmines.

The economic incentives also distort the way digital platforms are built. Systems optimized for surveillance prioritize data extraction over well-being, engagement over truth, and prediction over privacy. Even small design choices—default settings, notification prompts, or interface colors—are calibrated to maximize behavioral transparency. Companies do not need to force people to comply; they design environments where compliance feels natural.

Another consequence is that inequality deepens. Those who control surveillance networks—large technology companies, data brokers, and intelligence alliances—accumulate disproportionate power. Individuals, meanwhile, lose bargaining power because they cannot participate in society without generating data. Opting out means forfeiting access to communication, commerce, employment, and community. In this economic structure, surveillance is not a choice; it is the cost of modern citizenship.

Internationally, nations now compete for dominance in data infrastructure. Controlling cloud systems, social platforms, undersea cables, and AI models becomes a form of geopolitical leverage. Countries with the largest data streams wield disproportionate influence in global markets and security negotiations. Surveillance capitalism scales into surveillance geopolitics.

The long-term danger lies not only in privacy erosion but in the transformation of human autonomy. When companies and governments derive profit from predicting behavior, the line between prediction and manipulation blurs. If your future choices are economically valuable, systems will inevitably try to shape them. Free will becomes something exercised within pre-engineered boundaries—options that feel personal but are curated by invisible economic interests.

Yet critique alone is insufficient. The economics of watching persist because they solve problems efficiently: they personalize experiences, reduce friction, and create convenience. People willingly trade data for comfort because the consequences feel abstract compared to the immediate rewards. Surveillance survives not through coercion but through seduction.

In essence, the economics of watching represent a new social contract—one not openly negotiated, but silently accepted. We receive connectivity, personalization, and digital life. In return, we surrender visibility into our inner worlds. The most valuable commodity of the twenty-first century is not oil, minerals, or intellectual property—it is the human being rendered transparent. The challenge ahead is determining whether a transparent society can remain a free one.

Behavioral Engineering Through Data

Behavioral engineering—the deliberate shaping of human choices, emotions, and actions through data—has become one of the most powerful and least understood forces of the digital age. Unlike traditional manipulation, which relied on persuasion or coercion, behavioral engineering operates quietly beneath consciousness. It uses patterns extracted from millions of data points to design environments where people are predictably nudged toward certain behaviors. In this world, influence is not applied; it is embedded. People rarely realize they are being guided because the guidance feels like their own decision.

The foundation of behavioral engineering lies in the precision of modern data collection. Every digital interaction—likes, pauses, scrolls, purchases, hesitations—reveals micro-patterns about personality and motivation. Algorithms convert these patterns into behavioral maps, identifying what captures attention, what triggers fear, what prompts sharing, or what stimulates desire. These insights become blueprints for shaping future behavior. Platforms do not need to guess what people will do next; they can design environments that make that behavior highly probable.

One of the earliest and most widespread examples is the architecture of social media feeds. Content is not arranged chronologically but algorithmically. Each post, video, or image is chosen to maximize emotional engagement based on the user's psychological profile. This is not accidental. Behavioral engineering aims to evoke responses that prolong engagement, because engagement generates data, and data strengthens predictive accuracy. People believe they browse freely, yet every swipe is calibrated to guide them deeper into engineered emotional states—outrage, amusement, longing, tribal belonging. These states make behavior more predictable and therefore more valuable.

In commercial settings, behavioral engineering optimizes purchasing behavior. Companies analyze not only what consumers buy but *why* they buy—tracking the conditions that lead to impulse decisions. Pricing strategies, limited-time offers, interface colors, and even the sequence of options are crafted to subtly influence decisions. A consumer may think they purchased an item spontaneously, but in reality the environment was engineered to produce that impulse. The line between preference and manipulation blurs until it becomes nearly invisible.

Political actors have also embraced behavioral engineering. Campaign strategists use data-driven targeting to craft messages tailored to micro-demographics—offering different emotional triggers to different groups based on their fears, values, or grievances. Voters feel personally addressed because the messages resonate with their internal narratives.

Yet the resonance is algorithmically manufactured. Instead of persuading through debate, behavioral engineering shapes political identity through digital conditioning. Elections become less about public discourse and more about psychological segmentation.

The most profound aspect of behavioral engineering is its shift from reactive to proactive influence. Early digital systems responded to user behavior. Modern systems anticipate and modify it. Predictive algorithms detect when a user is vulnerable—bored, lonely, anxious, or receptive—and adjust content accordingly. They reinforce existing beliefs, intensify cravings, or push users toward actions aligned with the platform's goals. This anticipatory design transforms technology from a tool into an environment of constant psychological modulation.

What makes behavioral engineering particularly potent is its subtlety. Unlike propaganda or censorship, it does not restrict choices; it reframes them. People still feel free, because they are not forced—they are nudged. But repeated nudging accumulates into patterned behavior. Over time, individuals mistake engineered impulses for authentic desires. Autonomy becomes performative, not substantive.

There is also a collective dimension. When millions of people are nudged simultaneously, societal behavior shifts. Trends erupt, movements accelerate, divisions intensify, and public opinion swings with unprecedented speed. Behavioral engineering not only shapes individuals; it shapes cultures. It creates synchronized emotional waves—bursts of outrage, excitement, fear—that ripple through populations. These waves influence markets, elections, and social stability. The most powerful actors are not those who speak the loudest but those who control the algorithms that determine what is heard.

The ethical challenge arises from the asymmetry of power. Those being engineered do not know the rules; those engineering behavior do not have to justify their methods. Transparency is minimal because transparency undermines effectiveness. If people recognized how often their choices were shaped by invisible systems, they might resist. The system relies on ignorance to function.

Yet behavioral engineering is not inherently harmful. It can encourage healthy habits, reinforce learning, reduce energy use, or promote civic engagement. The question is not whether behavioral engineering should exist—it already does—but who controls it, for what purpose, and with what safeguards.

The deeper concern is existential. When data-driven systems can shape what people want before they know they want it, human agency becomes a contested space. The struggle of the future is not simply for privacy or free speech; it is for cognitive sovereignty—the ability to recognize where one's own mind ends and the machine's influence begins.

Behavioral engineering through data is the quiet architecture of modern power. It does not overthrow institutions; it rewires individuals. Understanding it is the first step toward reclaiming choice in a world designed to shape it.

Power in an Age Without Privacy

Privacy once functioned as a buffer between the individual and the world—a space for reflection, dissent, intimacy, and experimentation. It protected the fragile processes through which people form identity and make independent choices. But as the digital age accelerates, privacy dissolves into a luxury that few can afford and even fewer understand. What emerges in its absence is a new architecture of power—one that does not rely on censorship, coercion, or violence, but on visibility. When every action, preference, and hesitation becomes observable, predictability becomes total, and power becomes absolute.

The erosion of privacy is not the result of a single force but a convergence of many. Surveillance cameras map physical movement. Smartphones track location, conversations, sleep, and biometrics. Social platforms archive thoughts, friendships, and emotional states. E-commerce systems monitor desires. Governments integrate these streams into security infrastructures, while corporations use them as profit engines. The individual becomes transparent, rendered into data points that expose vulnerabilities long before they are consciously known.

In such a world, power shifts to those who control the mechanisms of observation. This control grants not only knowledge but influence—subtle, pervasive, and often invisible. When institutions know what people fear, what they crave, and what they avoid, they can shape environments that steer behavior without overt command. The old model of authority—laws, punishments, public decrees—becomes secondary to a quieter and more effective force: the manipulation of context.

The disappearance of privacy also alters the psychology of the citizen. When people feel watched, even abstractly, they modify their behavior. They become cautious, compliant, performative. They curate their identities to avoid judgment, penalties, or suspicion. This "internalized surveillance" is the ultimate efficiency for those in power: people police themselves. The cost of dissent becomes not only social but algorithmic. Speaking out risks being flagged, deprioritized, or categorized. Silence becomes self-preservation.

A society without privacy also redistributes fear. In previous eras, people feared external punishment. In the digital era, they fear being misunderstood by systems that do not explain their logic. Algorithms sort, categorize, and label individuals in ways they cannot challenge. A misinterpreted pattern of behavior can affect employment, credit, travel, or security status. Power is no longer personal but procedural—embedded in models that operate automatically. The most consequential decisions may be made by systems with no accountability.

And yet, the most profound consequence of a world without privacy is the collapse of unpredictability. Human beings are at their most creative, intuitive, and morally courageous when they act outside the gaze of authority. Privacy has historically allowed people to change their minds, test new beliefs, question norms, and rebel when necessary. Without privacy, dissent becomes traceable from its earliest spark. Movements are disrupted before they organize. Leaders are targeted before they rise. Ideas are contained before they transform the world. When unpredictability disappears, innovation and rebellion fade with it.

This transition produces a new kind of political order—one where control is distributed through networks instead of institutions. Power resides with those who hold the data, write the algorithms, and manage the infrastructure through which citizens interact with the world. Governments and corporations become intertwined, not through conspiracy but through dependence. One provides security; the other provides data. Together, they construct an environment in which visibility is constant and autonomy increasingly conditional.

Some argue that privacy must be sacrificed for safety or convenience. But safety without privacy becomes supervision, and convenience without privacy becomes behavioral conditioning. The trade-off is not merely technological; it is civilizational. A world without privacy becomes a world where the human spirit is subtly steered into predictability.

Yet the loss of privacy is not destiny. Societies can rebuild boundaries—through law, architecture, encryption, decentralized systems, and cultural resistance. The challenge is not restoring privacy as it once existed but redefining it in a world transformed by data. Power in an age without privacy is not immutable; it is simply the default. And defaults can be rewritten.

The future depends on whether people accept transparency as inevitable or demand systems that preserve the essential freedom to grow, question, and dissent beyond the gaze of authority. In that choice lies the difference between a managed population and a truly autonomous society.

CHAPTER 10

THE GLOBAL POWER SHIFT

The balance of global power is never fixed. It bends, contracts, fractures, and reorganizes itself as civilizations rise, mature, and decline. Today, the world stands at one of the most significant turning points since the end of World War II. The economic and political dominance long held by Western powers is weakening, not through sudden collapse but through gradual erosion—an accumulation of internal strain, external competition, and shifting global priorities. Meanwhile, new powers are asserting themselves with confidence, reshaping the contours of influence across continents.

This transition is not defined by a single event but by a constellation of pressures: demographic shifts, technological revolutions, resource scarcity, debt crises, regional conflicts, and ideological realignments. Traditional empires are discovering that their institutions, once symbols of stability, are struggling to adapt to a world moving faster than their political systems can respond. At the same time, rising nations—particularly those in Asia, Africa, and parts of the Middle East—are leveraging youthful populations, strategic geography, and ambitious economic programs to expand their influence.

The global landscape now resembles a mosaic rather than a hierarchy. Power is distributed across state actors, multinational corporations, financial blocs, and technological networks. Economic alliances—built around energy, infrastructure, digital connectivity, and resource security—are replacing older military-centered coalitions. The world is not becoming leaderless; it is becoming multipolar, with competing visions for how the future should be governed.

This chapter examines the decline of old empires, the rise of new hegemons, and the evolving alliances redefining global strategy. Understanding this shift is essential, because the emerging order will shape how nations negotiate conflict, share resources, build economies, and respond to the cascading crises of the twenty-first century.

The Decline of Old Empires

The decline of old empires is rarely dramatic at first. It begins quietly, almost imperceptibly, as cracks form beneath the surface of institutions that once appeared unshakable. For decades, Western powers—particularly the United States and the longstanding European empires—shaped global economics, security frameworks, and cultural narratives. Their dominance was so extensive that it seemed permanent, a natural order rather than a historical phase. Yet like every previous empire, their influence now wanes not through sudden collapse but through gradual exhaustion, internal contradictions, and the emergence of competitors better adapted to a transformed world.

One of the earliest signs of imperial decline is institutional stagnation. Systems that once facilitated innovation become resistant to change. Political structures designed for earlier eras struggle to cope with twenty-first-century challenges: immigration flows, digital disruption, demographic aging, and economic inequality. Rather than adapt, institutions cling to tradition, producing gridlock, polarization, and public distrust. The energy that once fueled expansion turns inward, consumed by internal friction.

Economic pressures intensify the decline. Western economies built their prosperity on industrial manufacturing, global trade networks, and post-war financial dominance. But manufacturing shifted abroad, supply chains globalized beyond their control, and financial systems became increasingly fragile. Debt levels soar, middle classes shrink, and younger generations inherit stagnant wages and diminished opportunities. The economic engines that once powered empire slow down, reducing not only domestic confidence but global leverage.

At the same time, demographic shifts reshape geopolitical capacity. Many old empires face aging populations, declining birth rates, and strained social support systems. A shrinking workforce limits growth and innovation. Military recruitment becomes harder, welfare burdens expand, and national energy dissipates. Demographics, once a source of strength, now constrain ambition.

Cultural influence also fades. Western soft power—rooted in media, education, technology, and cultural prestige—is challenged by rising nations projecting their own narratives. As alternative models of governance and development gain visibility, Western values no longer carry the universal authority they once claimed. Nations previously aligned with Western interests explore new partnerships, decreasing reliance on old empires and eroding their cultural reach.

Another dimension of decline is strategic overextension. Like many historical empires, Western powers invested heavily in military presence across the globe. Maintaining bases, interventions, and security commitments becomes increasingly costly and politically unpopular. Domestic populations grow weary of endless conflicts, questioning their purpose and benefit. This reluctance signals to the world that the empire's appetite for global policing is diminishing. Competitors observe these hesitations and move into spaces once dominated by Western influence.

Diplomatic authority weakens as well. The institutions the West built—international courts, trade bodies, alliances—lose legitimacy when the world perceives them as outdated or biased. When rising powers push back, old empires can no longer dictate the rules. Their ability to shape global norms diminishes as the international order becomes multipolar, with competing visions of governance.

Technological leadership, once a Western monopoly, is no longer assured. Other nations now spearhead advancements in artificial intelligence, quantum computing, energy innovation, and digital infrastructure. The global center of technological gravity shifts, leaving old empires reliant on systems they no longer fully control. This loss of innovation dominance weakens both economic influence and military capacity.

Energy transitions further expose vulnerabilities. As the world shifts toward renewable systems, countries historically dependent on fossil-fuel economics struggle to reinvent themselves fast enough. Infrastructure built for earlier centuries becomes obsolete. Transition costs strain budgets, testing political cohesion and accelerating decline.

However, the decline of old empires is not equivalent to disappearance. Empires rarely vanish—they transform. Influence becomes selective rather than universal. Power becomes negotiated rather than imposed.

Instead of commanding global systems, old empires must compete within them. The decline is not merely a fall from greatness; it is a recalibration of relevance in a world that no longer centers them.

The most profound aspect of this decline is psychological. Societies accustomed to dominance struggle to adjust to relative parity. Nostalgia replaces vision. Political movements arise that promise restoration rather than adaptation. This inward search for identity further reduces global engagement and accelerates strategic retreat. A civilization unsure of its future cannot confidently shape the future of others.

The decline of old empires does not signal global chaos but a shift toward distributed power. As their dominance fades, new actors rise—regional powers, technology blocs, economic alliances—creating a more complex and unpredictable global landscape. What follows is not the end of influence for old empires but the end of automatic authority. Their future depends on whether they cling to past identities or reinvent themselves for a world they no longer singularly define.

The Emergence of New Hegemonies

The waning influence of old empires has created a power vacuum—a rare geopolitical opening in which new hegemons are rising with remarkable speed and strategic clarity. Unlike previous global powers, these emerging states and blocs do not model themselves on Western imperial traditions. Their ascent is shaped by demographics, technology, resource strategy, and economic ambition rather than colonial conquest. They rise not through dominance of territory, but through dominance of infrastructure, supply chains, digital ecosystems, and regional influence. Their hegemony is quieter, more networked, and more adaptive to the complexities of the modern world.

At the center of this shift is China. Its rise is not sudden but the result of decades of deliberate state planning, population strength, industrial discipline, and technological investment. China's influence spreads through trade rather than occupation, through ports instead of bases, through digital innovation instead of ideology. The Belt and Road Initiative extends its reach across Africa, Asia, Europe, and the Middle East, creating economic dependencies that translate into political leverage.

Beijing's strategy is not to replace Western hegemons with a replica of their system, but to redefine global leadership around supply-chain dominance, manufacturing control, and financial influence.

India emerges through a different model—population scale, digital infrastructure, and cultural expansion. With the world's largest workforce and a rapidly developing technological sector, India positions itself as a balancing power between East and West. Its influence grows through alliances in the Indo-Pacific, leadership in the Global South, and the projection of soft power through diaspora, media, and democratic appeal. India's ambition is not to mirror China's centralized model, but to leverage its demographic advantage and strategic geography to become an indispensable node in global economics and security.

Regional hegemons also gain prominence in ways that reflect their unique capabilities. Turkey expands influence through geography, military capacity, and diplomatic agility across Europe, the Middle East, and Central Asia. Brazil leverages agricultural dominance and resource wealth to shape South American stability and global food systems. Nigeria, with its vast population and energy potential, positions itself as a central force in West Africa's emerging economic corridors. Iran, Saudi Arabia, and the UAE use energy wealth, religious influence, and financial power to reshape Middle Eastern politics while forging unconventional strategic partnerships.

What distinguishes many of these emerging powers is their comfort with multipolarity. Instead of aligning exclusively with old blocs, they build flexible relationships. China partners with Russia for energy, yet invests deeply in Africa. India collaborates with the United States on defense while maintaining economic ties with Iran. Middle Eastern states diversify alliances among Europe, Asia, and global corporations. This fluid diplomacy allows new hegemons to avoid entanglements that weakened older empires.

Technology accelerates their rise. Control over data, artificial intelligence, telecommunications infrastructure, and digital payment systems becomes more decisive than control over traditional military power. Nations investing heavily in AI, cyber capabilities, and digital governance establish influence that extends beyond borders. Digital hegemony—

unlike territorial hegemony—can reach every household on the planet. China's 5G networks, India's digital ID systems, and Gulf states' investments in smart cities demonstrate how deeply new hegemonies embed themselves into the daily lives of billions.

Economic strategy also plays a critical role. Emerging powers excel at resource diplomacy—acquiring farmland abroad, securing mining rights, investing in energy corridors, and building infrastructure that ensures long-term access. These moves are not signs of empire-building but of survival in a world of scarcity. By controlling resource flows, they secure leverage that older powers increasingly lack. Their influence grows not through coercion but through indispensability.

Culturally, new hegemonies rise through media, entertainment, education exchanges, and linguistic influence. Korean pop culture shapes global youth identity. Indian cinema reaches more viewers than Hollywood in many regions. Chinese universities attract tens of thousands of international students. These soft-power channels strengthen global familiarity and acceptance, reinforcing geopolitical influence.

However, the emergence of new hegemons is not without tension. Their ambitions often overlap, creating zones of competition in the Indo-Pacific, Africa, Central Asia, and cyberspace. But unlike the bipolar Cold War era, today's competition is diffuse, pragmatic, and often economic rather than ideological. These rising powers understand that influence in the twenty-first century is earned through relevance, not conquest.

In a depleted and interconnected world, new hegemonies thrive by mastering adaptation—shifting alliances, technological acceleration, and resource strategy. Their ascent signals not merely a change in who leads the world but a transformation in what leadership means. The future global order will not revolve around a single empire but around multiple centers of gravity, each shaping civilization in its own image.

Economic Alliances Reshaping the World

Economic alliances are becoming the new engines of global power, reshaping geopolitics more profoundly than military coalitions ever could. As traditional empires weaken and multipolarity rises, nations recognize that influence in the twenty-first century depends less on territorial control and more on integration—of markets, infrastructure, technology, and financial systems. These alliances do not simply promote trade; they redefine strategic priorities, redirect flows of capital, and redraw the world's economic map. In a fractured and resource-scarce world, partnerships become a form of survival, a hedge against volatility, and a pathway to new forms of dominance.

The most visible example of this shift is the reconfiguration of global economic blocs. Organizations such as BRICS evolve from loose associations into platforms for financial independence and political cooperation. Their expansion—bringing in new members from Asia, Africa, and the Middle East—signals the rise of a counterweight to Western institutions. These alliances seek to reduce reliance on the U.S. dollar, diversify trade routes, and develop alternative banking systems. Their goal is not merely economic integration but sovereignty: the ability to operate outside frameworks built by older powers.

Traditional alliances, meanwhile, face pressure to reinvent themselves. Economic structures like the European Union struggle with internal fragmentation, demographic decline, and uneven growth. Yet they remain significant players because of their regulatory power and innovation capacity. The EU's influence increasingly comes from "rule-setting hegemony"—its ability to shape global standards on data, trade, privacy, and environmental policy. In a world where supply chains span continents, whoever sets the rules holds subtle but decisive power.

Asia becomes the gravitational center of new alliances. Regional partnerships such as the Regional Comprehensive Economic Partnership (RCEP) form enormous trade networks that bind together manufacturing hubs, technology centers, and consumer markets. These alliances strengthen regional autonomy and reduce dependency on Western markets. They also allow emerging powers to negotiate from positions of collective strength rather than isolated vulnerability. The Indo-Pacific, once a peripheral theater, becomes the new global economic heartland.

Infrastructure alliances also reshape global power. China's Belt and Road Initiative is the most ambitious project of this kind, linking ports, highways, energy corridors, and digital networks across dozens of countries. These projects create long-term economic dependency while embedding

Chinese influence into the physical and technological foundations of partner nations. But China is not alone. Gulf states invest heavily in African infrastructure, Japan builds strategic connectivity in Southeast Asia, and India extends energy and transport corridors across neighboring regions. Infrastructure is no longer just construction—it is diplomacy by steel and concrete.

Energy alliances take on heightened significance as the world transitions away from fossil fuels. Nations rich in lithium, cobalt, nickel, and rare earth minerals form strategic partnerships with those who possess manufacturing capacity or technological expertise. Meanwhile, states with strong renewable potential—solar-rich deserts, wind-heavy coastlines, geothermal regions—create energy-sharing agreements that secure long-term stability. The global race for battery technology and green hydrogen further knits together states in new patterns of interdependence. The alliances born from these transitions will determine who leads the next industrial era.

Digital alliances represent another frontier. Nations link their futures through shared cybersecurity frameworks, data governance agreements, and AI-development partnerships. Whoever controls the architecture of digital trade controls the arteries of global communication and commerce. Digital alliances also strengthen power through exclusion: states outside these networks find themselves technologically isolated, economically disadvantaged, and politically vulnerable. In a world where information is wealth, digital partnerships become the new treaties of power.

Financial alliances reshape the global monetary landscape. Nations diversify reserves, adopt dual-currency settlement systems, and experiment with central bank digital currencies (CBDCs) to bypass traditional banking networks. These changes weaken the monopoly of Western financial institutions and introduce a more fluid, competitive monetary system. Whether this creates stability or fragmentation remains uncertain, but the shift is undeniable.

What makes modern economic alliances transformative is their multidimensional nature. They do not exist solely for trade; they shape migration, technology flows, environmental strategies, and political alignments. Power no longer resides in dominance over others but in being indispensable to a network—an anchor within a web of interdependencies. Nations that integrate deeply into alliances gain resilience; those that remain isolated face volatility and decline.

In a world defined by scarcity, climate disruption, and rapid technological change, alliances become shields, leverage points, and identity markers. They determine not only who thrives but who survives. Economic alliances are no longer technical arrangements—they are the architecture of the new world order, silently redrawing the lines of power for the century ahead.

CHAPTER 11
HUMANITY AT THE THRESHOLD

Humanity stands at a threshold unlike any it has faced before. Economic systems strain under global pressures, technological power grows faster than moral imagination, and climate instability challenges the foundations of daily life. Yet this moment is not defined only by danger—it is defined by choice. Civilizations throughout history have confronted turning points, moments when their values, actions, and collective decisions determined whether they advanced, transformed, or collapsed. Today, humanity faces such a crossroads on a planetary scale.

The forces shaping this era are profound: automation that redefines human purpose, surveillance that dissolves privacy, resource scarcity that reshapes geopolitics, and inequality that corrodes social cohesion. These developments present ethical questions that older systems were never designed to answer. What should progress serve—profit, power, or human flourishing? How much control should institutions hold over individual lives? How does a civilization maintain dignity when technology can predict, influence, and replace human behavior?

Yet alongside these pressures lies unparalleled potential. Humans have the knowledge to prevent collapse, the creativity to reinvent systems, and the capacity for solidarity even amid fragmentation. The future is neither guaranteed nor predetermined. It will emerge from a delicate tension between fear and aspiration, despair and possibility.

This chapter explores three dimensions of this threshold moment: the ethical crossroads that define the coming era, the psychological and social struggle between hope and despair, and the deeper question of what civilization ultimately chooses to become. The choices societies make now—about governance, technology, resource use, and moral responsibility—will shape not only the fate of nations, but the character of humanity itself.

Ethical Crossroads of the Coming Era

Humanity is entering an era defined not by the limits of technology, but by the limits of conscience. Never before have societies possessed tools capable of reshaping life, governance, and identity at such staggering scales. Automation, artificial intelligence, genetic engineering, digital surveillance, and climate manipulation each promise profound benefits—but they also pose ethical challenges that strike at the core of what it means to be human. At this crossroads, technological capability has outpaced moral clarity. The coming decades will test not only innovation but judgment, restraint, and collective wisdom.

One of the most urgent ethical dilemmas concerns autonomy. As AI systems influence decisions in finance, healthcare, policing, employment, and relationships, individuals risk losing agency over their own lives. When algorithms predict behavior better than people understand themselves, the boundary between guidance and coercion becomes blurred. Should institutions be allowed to shape public behavior for efficiency, safety, or profit? Or does such shaping violate fundamental human rights, even when it appears beneficial? The choice is not simply about privacy—it is about sovereignty of thought.

Economically, societies must confront the ethical consequences of automation. Machines replacing human labor raises deep questions: What happens to people whose skills become obsolete? Do governments have a responsibility to guarantee livelihoods in a post-work economy? Should wealth generated by automation belong to corporations, the state, or the broader population? These questions are not merely technical; they concern fairness, dignity, and the moral duty of a civilization to its most vulnerable members.

In the realm of biotechnology, humanity faces choices that previous generations could not even imagine. Gene editing may eliminate hereditary diseases, but it could also lead to engineered inequality—where genetic enhancement becomes a luxury for the wealthy. Should society permit the modification of human embryos? Who decides which traits are acceptable or desirable? At stake is not just medical progress but the definition of human identity itself. When technology can redesign the human blueprint, ethics becomes the last line of defense against creating hierarchies written into biology.

Environmental ethics also enter a new phase. With climate instability threatening food systems, migration patterns, and political stability, some nations consider radical interventions—geoengineering, synthetic weather control, and large-scale carbon manipulation. These strategies may buy time, but they also involve enormous risks. Who controls the global thermostat? What happens if technological fixes benefit some regions while harming others? Ethical stewardship must extend beyond national borders, demanding a planetary perspective in which the well-being of future generations is weighed against the urgency of present crises.

Surveillance and information control introduce another ethical battlefield. Digital footprints expose intimate details about individuals' beliefs, behaviors, and vulnerabilities. As governments and corporations accumulate unprecedented insight into human psychology, the temptation to shape or limit dissent grows stronger. Should societies accept surveillance as the cost of security? Or must they defend the right to opacity, unpredictability, and dissent even at the risk of vulnerability? The ethical argument here is profound: a society without privacy cannot sustain true freedom.

Global inequality further complicates every ethical question. Technologies that promise to elevate humanity may instead deepen divides between nations and classes. The ethical challenge is not only distributing tools fairly, but ensuring that innovation does not become a new form of imperialism—where wealthy nations engineer progress for themselves while poorer regions suffer ecological damage, economic stagnation, or political manipulation. A just future requires designing systems that uplift rather than exclude.

Underlying all these dilemmas is the question of responsibility. Who decides how powerful technologies are used? Who bears the consequences when they fail? The traditional guardians of ethics—religion, philosophy, democratic debate—struggle to keep pace with exponential change. At the crossroads of the coming era, humanity must develop new frameworks capable of bridging technology and morality, innovation and compassion.

The danger is not merely choosing wrongly, but choosing passively—allowing momentum, convenience, or corporate interests to dictate decisions that shape civilization. Ethical crossroads demand active, intentional deliberation. They require societies to articulate what they value: freedom or control, equality or efficiency, human complexity or engineered predictability.

The coming era will not be defined by what technology allows us to do, but by what humanity decides it must *not* do, even when the power exists. Ethics becomes the compass that prevents civilization from drifting into futures that are technologically impressive but spiritually hollow. The crossroads is here—and what humanity chooses will echo through generations.

The Struggle Between Hope and Despair

Every era of upheaval forces humanity into an emotional battleground where hope and despair collide. In times of rapid transformation, people instinctively search for meaning, stability, and reassurance. Yet the same conditions that spark innovation and resilience also magnify fear, uncertainty, and fatigue. The struggle between hope and despair is not a philosophical abstraction—it is a lived psychological reality shaping how individuals, communities, and nations respond to crisis. This tension becomes especially pronounced when old systems falter and new ones are not yet formed.

Despair emerges from fragmentation. When people feel their future slipping beyond their control, they tend to see the world through a shrinking lens. Economic insecurity, technological overwhelm, political instability, and environmental anxiety combine to create a sense of inevitability—a belief that decline is irreversible. Despair thrives in silence, growing strongest when individuals feel isolated or unheard. It feeds on narratives of collapse, amplifying every failure until human agency starts to look like an illusion rather than a force.

Hope, however, is not the naive counterpart of despair; it is a form of disciplined imagination. Hope requires the courage to envision possibilities beyond immediate conditions. Unlike optimism, which assumes things will improve, hope acknowledges struggle while insisting that change remains possible through effort and collective will. Hope is active. It resists paralysis. It invites participation in shaping outcomes rather than waiting for forces beyond one's control to dictate them.

The psychological battle between these two forces intensifies when institutions lose credibility. When governments, financial systems, religious authorities, and social structures fail to deliver stability or justice, despair finds fertile ground. In such periods, people may drift toward fatalistic thinking, conspiracy frameworks, or extreme movements that promise clarity amid chaos. Despair simplifies the world into rigid binaries—us versus them, destruction versus salvation. It numbs critical thought and replaces complexity with absolutes.

Yet crises also reveal the surprising durability of human resilience. Throughout history—during plagues, wars, famines, and revolutions—hope has surfaced in unexpected places. Communities reimagined themselves. Individuals discovered capacities they never recognized. Deep transformation often arises from moments when despair appears overwhelming. Part of this resilience comes from humanity's narrative instinct: the ability to make sense of suffering by embedding it within broader stories of purpose, redemption, or renewal. Whether grounded in faith, philosophy, or personal memory, these stories allow people to endure the present without surrendering the future.

Modern society, however, complicates this struggle. Digital environments magnify despair by accelerating the spread of negative information, amplifying outrage, and eroding attention spans. Constant exposure to global crises—economic downturns, climate disasters, wars, and technological disruption—creates an atmosphere of chronic emotional fatigue. People begin to internalize collapse as a permanent condition. Under such pressure, hope can feel like an act of rebellion rather than an emotional state.

At the same time, the digital age also nurtures hope in unprecedented ways. Ideas travel faster, coalitions form more easily, and marginalized voices can challenge dominant narratives. Innovations in medicine, education, communication, and clean energy demonstrate that solutions are not hypothetical—they are already unfolding. Hope grows stronger when people witness progress in real time, even if uneven and incomplete. The visibility of global cooperation, scientific breakthroughs, and social reform movements provides a counterweight to despair's gravitational pull.

The struggle between hope and despair becomes most significant when societies stand on the threshold of transformation. Despair pushes people toward withdrawal, cynicism, or surrender. Hope pushes them toward engagement, problem-solving, and collective creativity. Each force shapes decisions that ripple outward—politically, economically, and culturally. A population consumed by despair demands fewer possibilities. A population sustained by hope becomes capable of imagining new systems, new values, and new forms of coexistence.

Ultimately, the conflict between hope and despair reveals a deeper truth about civilization: the future is not dictated solely by external events but by how humanity chooses to interpret and respond to them. Despair narrows vision; hope widens it. Despair convinces people they are powerless; hope reminds them they are participants in the story of their time. The struggle is ongoing, but not symmetrical—because even a small, persistent act of hope can disrupt a vast structure of despair.

The destiny of any civilization depends on which force it cultivates. At the threshold of a new era, the question is not whether challenges will arise—they will. The real question is whether humanity will face them with resignation or with the courage to imagine something better.

What Civilization Chooses to Become

Civilization is not a passive outcome of history—it is an active construction shaped by the choices societies make under pressure. When old systems begin to fracture and uncertainty defines the horizon, humanity is forced to confront a profound question: *What kind of world do we want to create?* This question becomes unavoidable in moments of global transition, when technological revolutions, environmental instability, demographic shifts, and geopolitical realignments converge. At such thresholds, the future is neither inherited nor inevitable. It becomes a deliberate moral and strategic project.

Every civilization eventually reaches a reflective moment when it must choose between competing visions of itself. One direction is shaped by fear: the desire for security at any cost, the retreat into nationalism, authoritarian structures, and rigid identities. This path promises order but delivers stagnation. It often sacrifices human dignity for the illusion of control. The other direction is shaped by courage: a willingness to evolve, to reexamine foundational assumptions, and to redesign systems that no longer serve the public good. This second path is more difficult because it requires imagination, humility, and collective effort—qualities that often feel in short supply during crisis.

Modern society faces choices previous generations never encountered. For the first time in history, humanity possesses tools capable of altering consciousness, biology, climate, and global governance. Such power demands ethical maturity. The question is not whether civilization *can* push forward technologically—it inevitably will. The question is whether its moral development will keep pace, guiding progress rather than being overshadowed by it. Without ethical alignment, power becomes fragmentation; with it, power becomes a catalyst for renewal.

One of the central choices concerns the value of human life in an age of automation and digital influence. Civilization can choose to treat people as data points—resources to manage, predict, and optimize. Or it can choose to reaffirm human agency as the core of societal purpose. This decision will shape policies on education, labor, governance, and technology. If civilization decides that efficiency outweighs dignity, it risks creating a world where meaning erodes. But if it chooses to cultivate human creativity, empathy, and autonomy, technology can become an extension of humanity rather than its replacement.

Another choice lies in how societies respond to inequality. A world drifting toward extreme wealth concentration invites instability, resentment, and fragmentation. Yet the tools exist to distribute opportunity more widely. Civilization can choose extractive systems that benefit the few, or regenerative systems that sustain communities, ecosystems, and future generations. The structure of economies is not a natural law—it is a collective decision. And decisions can be reimagined.

Environmental collapse presents another defining choice. The planet will recover with or without humans; the real question is whether humanity chooses to live in harmony with ecological limits or continues to exhaust them. A civilization that values short-term benefit over long-term survival is not a civilization planning for its future. Conversely, a world that recognizes interdependence—between humans, technology, and nature—can become more resilient than any past society.

Culturally, civilization must decide what it means to belong. Will societies fragment into polarized tribes defined by misinformation, identity conflict, and digital isolation? Or will they seek new forms of shared meaning that transcend borders and ideologies? The future of culture depends on whether humanity embraces connection or retreats into suspicion. Even in an age of hyper-individualism, civilizations endure through cooperation, shared narratives, and mutual responsibility.

Perhaps the most profound choice is philosophical: whether humanity views itself as a species in decline or a species in transformation. If civilization internalizes a narrative of doom, it will act accordingly—defensively, narrowly, destructively. But if it embraces the possibility of renewal, it can rewrite its trajectory. Crisis can be catalyst. Collapse can clear space for reinvention. The future is neither pre-written nor guaranteed; it is shaped by collective imagination and collective will.

Ultimately, what civilization chooses to become depends on the stories it tells about itself. Stories of fear produce walls; stories of possibility produce bridges. Stories of scarcity lead to conflict; stories of shared destiny lead to collaboration. The coming era demands not just new technologies or political reforms, but a redefinition of what it means to thrive as a species.

Civilization stands at a turning point where survival and evolution are equally possible. The question that remains—one only humanity can answer—is whether we will choose a future built on fear or a future built on responsibility, vision, and courage. The path forward is open. What we become is up to us.

CHAPTER 12
BUILDING A FUTURE BEYOND SURVIVAL

Civilizations rarely collapse in a single moment. They unravel slowly, thread by thread, until the world that once felt permanent becomes a memory. Yet history also shows that collapse is not the end of human possibility—it is the clearing of a path. When familiar systems fail, humanity gains a rare chance to rethink its assumptions, rebuild its priorities, and design a future not bound by the limitations of the past. This chapter explores that pivotal opportunity: how societies can move beyond mere survival and begin constructing a world that is not only sustainable but meaningful.

The twenty-first century forces a stark reckoning with the consequences of centuries of extraction, inequality, and unchecked growth. But it also reveals extraordinary potential for reinvention. As old economic models fracture, new forms of prosperity—rooted in balance rather than exploitation—begin to take shape. As global governance struggles under the weight of crisis, new moral frameworks emerge that prioritize human dignity, ecological responsibility, and long-term resilience. And as individuals confront uncertainty, they rediscover collective strength, creativity, and the will to reimagine what a civilization can be.

Building a future beyond survival requires more than technological fixes or temporary policies. It demands a fundamental shift in the stories societies tell about wealth, progress, and human purpose. It involves designing systems where prosperity does not depend on depletion, where security does not require domination, and where value is measured not only by markets but by well-being and stewardship.

This chapter examines three pillars of that transformation: how prosperity can be redefined without exploitation, what a new moral foundation for global systems might look like, and how economies could function in a world shaped by collapse yet open to renewal. The goal is not to predict the future, but to illuminate the choices that will shape it.

Reimagining Prosperity Without Exploitation

Prosperity has long been defined through a narrow lens—growth, accumulation, control, and the extraction of resources, both human and natural. For centuries, this model delivered extraordinary advances in technology, health, and global connectivity. Yet its hidden costs have become impossible to ignore. Ecological collapse, widespread inequality, and the erosion of social cohesion reveal the fundamental flaw in equating prosperity with unlimited expansion. To build a viable future, civilization must reformulate the meaning of prosperity itself. It must seek abundance without depletion, success without domination, and progress without sacrificing the well-being of people or the planet.

Reimagining prosperity begins with recognizing that exploitation—of land, labor, or communities—is not a feature of economic growth but a failure of imagination. Modern systems evolved from a worldview that treated the Earth as an infinite storehouse and people as interchangeable units of productivity. This mindset valued efficiency over dignity and extraction over regeneration. But as the consequences of that worldview become clearer, societies are beginning to explore models that honor limits and cultivate resilience instead of fragility.

One emerging idea is the regenerative economy. Unlike traditional systems that consume resources faster than they can be replenished, regenerative models restore what they use. They treat ecosystems as partners rather than commodities. Cities powered by renewable energy, agriculture that enriches soil instead of depleting it, and industries that design products for reuse instead of disposal represent not merely environmental reforms but a philosophical shift. Prosperity becomes measured by the long-term health of communities and landscapes—not by quarterly profits.

Human prosperity also requires redefining labor. In the old paradigm, work was primarily a means of survival, often disconnected from purpose or creativity. Many people spent their lives performing tasks that enriched a small elite while leaving them personally unfulfilled. A future without exploitation demands labor systems that honor agency, autonomy, and meaning. Technology, which once displaced workers, can instead be harnessed to reduce drudgery and expand human potential. If machines take over monotonous tasks, humans can focus on roles rooted in empathy, creativity, and problem-solving—capacities machines cannot authentically replicate.

Yet this shift requires more than technological optimism. It demands structural change. Universal basic income or other forms of social support may become essential as automation transforms the labor market. Such systems, however controversial, challenge the assumption that a person's value lies in their market productivity. Instead, they assert that human dignity is inherent. In a world where survival is no longer tied to wage labor, individuals could pursue education, caregiving, artistic expression, and community-building—activities vital to a flourishing society but undervalued in current economies.

Reimagined prosperity also requires confronting inequality. The concentration of wealth in the hands of a few is not simply a moral issue; it is an economic threat. Inequality weakens social trust, reduces economic stability, and undermines democratic institutions. A post-exploitation prosperity model redistributes opportunity—not through punitive measures but through systems that cultivate widespread empowerment. Fair taxation, public investment in education and healthcare, and policies that support small enterprises rather than corporate monopolies can create environments where prosperity is shared rather than hoarded.

In global terms, reimagining prosperity means rejecting historical patterns of exploitation that shaped relations between powerful and vulnerable nations. A future built on cooperation must move beyond extractive trade, resource theft, and debt traps. Instead, equitable partnerships, technology-sharing agreements, and collaborative environmental stewardship can create a global system where prosperity is mutually reinforcing rather than competitive. The question is not which nation gains the most, but how humanity as a whole benefits.

Cultural transformation is equally essential. For generations, societies have equated success with accumulation—bigger homes, more possessions, constant consumption. But research consistently shows that beyond a certain threshold, material wealth does little to increase happiness. What does foster well-being is connection, purpose, autonomy, and belonging. A civilization that values these qualities over perpetual consumption moves closer to a sustainable, life-enhancing definition of prosperity.

Ultimately, reimagining prosperity without exploitation is not a utopian dream. It is a survival strategy. The old model has reached its breaking point; continuing it guarantees ecological exhaustion and social collapse. But choosing a new path opens the possibility of a civilization that thrives without destroying itself. Prosperity becomes not the privilege of a few but the collective state of a society that protects its people, restores its ecosystems, and honors its moral responsibilities.

A future built on regeneration rather than extraction invites humanity to redefine what it means to live well. It asks us to imagine abundance without sacrifice—and to build systems where flourishing is shared, sustainable, and deeply human.

A New Moral Foundation for Global Systems

For centuries, global systems—economic, political, and technological—have been built on assumptions derived from conquest, competition, and extraction. These assumptions shaped the modern world, but they are now proving inadequate for a planet facing existential risks. The crises of the twenty-first century—climate instability, technological disruption, pandemics, mass inequality, and geopolitical fragmentation—cannot be navigated with frameworks designed for an earlier age. To build a future beyond mere survival, humanity must construct a new moral foundation for its global systems, one aligned with interdependence, responsibility, and long-term stewardship.

Such a foundation begins with a simple but profound recognition: the fate of each society is bound to the fate of all others. Traditional models treated nations as isolated competitors, each striving for dominance. Yet today, environmental collapse in one region can destabilize economies across oceans; a financial crisis in a single country can ripple into a worldwide recession; a technological breakthrough can alter power dynamics for billions. Interdependence is not a philosophical ideal but a material reality. A new moral framework must therefore emphasize shared responsibility rather than isolated self-interest.

At the heart of this transformation lies the concept of planetary ethics—a recognition that human systems cannot be divorced from ecological limits. For centuries, the natural world was treated as a backdrop to human progress, a reservoir of infinite resources. But environmental data reveals that continued exploitation guarantees collapse. A moral foundation for global systems must acknowledge that prosperity is impossible on a dying planet. This means embedding ecological regeneration into the core of economic architecture: industries that restore rather than degrade, policies that honor biodiversity, and technologies designed to harmonize with natural cycles rather than override them.

A second pillar of this new moral foundation is human dignity. Global systems have too often valued people for their economic output rather than their inherent worth. As automation and AI reshape labor markets, this old calculus becomes even more dangerous. If the future is to remain humane, systems must be redesigned to protect autonomy, elevate well-being, and ensure equitable access to opportunity. This involves rethinking education, healthcare, labor, and digital governance not as commodities but as rights. A moral global framework must insist that no technological advancement justifies the erosion of human dignity.

Third, justice must become a structural priority. Inequality is not an inevitable outcome of human society—it is a consequence of decisions made by institutions. Wealth concentration, resource theft, exploitative trade, and predatory financial systems shaped the world we inherited. A new moral foundation must confront these injustices directly. Fair taxation, transparent governance, ethical trade agreements, and anti-corruption mechanisms are not merely economic reforms—they are moral commitments. Justice also extends between nations. Former colonial powers and economic giants must recognize their historical advantages and work toward systems that uplift rather than exploit developing regions.

Fourth, the governance of technology demands a moral compass. Innovation without ethical oversight leads to manipulation, surveillance, and algorithmic bias. A global moral framework must ensure that technological power serves humanity rather than controls it. This means establishing international norms for AI development, protecting privacy, preventing digital authoritarianism, and ensuring that technological benefits are shared rather than monopolized by corporations or powerful states. Technology must amplify human potential, not diminish human freedom.

Another key element is collective truth. In an age of disinformation, conspiracy theories, and fragmented realities, global systems cannot function if societies cannot agree on basic facts. The erosion of truth corrodes democracy, destabilizes public health, and makes coordinated action almost impossible. A moral foundation must therefore include commitments to transparency, responsible media ecosystems, and education that cultivates critical thinking rather than blind consumption of information.

Perhaps the most transformative element of this new moral foundation is humility. For too long, global systems have operated under the assumption that growth is limitless, humans are separate from nature, and technology will solve every problem. Humility acknowledges limits—ecological, ethical, and existential. It requires leaders and institutions to recognize uncertainty, listen to marginalized voices, and adapt when evidence demands change. Humility does not weaken global systems; it makes them resilient.

Ultimately, a new moral foundation for global systems is not a theoretical exercise—it is a prerequisite for survival. Without a shift in underlying values, attempts to reform the economy, rebuild trust, or regulate technology will fail. But if civilizations embrace responsibility, dignity, justice, ecological harmony, and humility, they can design systems capable of weathering the storms ahead.

The future will not be defined by the sophistication of our tools, but by the strength of our moral imagination. Only when global systems rest on ethical foundations can humanity build a world that is not merely sustainable—but worthy of its own survival.

The Economics of a Post-Collapse World

When a civilization collapses, the familiar scaffolding of economic life—currencies, markets, institutions, supply chains—begins to disintegrate. But collapse does not eliminate economic activity; it transforms it. People still trade, share, build, and compete. They still allocate resources, negotiate value, and search for stability. The difference is that the assumptions underpinning the old system no longer apply. A post-collapse world forces societies to rethink what is essential, what is negotiable, and what prosperity truly means. In this environment, economics shifts from a system of expansion to a system of survival, regeneration, and reorientation.

The first transformation in a post-collapse economy is the revaluation of resources. When global systems fail, the commodities that once symbolized wealth—stocks, digital assets, vast landholdings, luxury goods—rapidly lose meaning. What becomes valuable is far more elemental: water, fertile soil, medicine, local energy sources, durable tools, and skilled labor. This shift exposes a truth that modern markets often conceal: the foundation of all wealth is ecological and human, not financial. Economies begin to reorganize around access to essentials rather than the accumulation of abstractions.

Currency itself may fracture or vanish. Trust in centralized financial authorities erodes, prompting communities to adopt barter systems, local tokens, time-based currencies, or digital alternatives not dependent on national governance. These systems emerge not out of idealism but necessity; they provide a means to coordinate exchange when broader financial networks no longer function. In some cases, multiple forms of currency coexist, each tied to different kinds of trust—social, communal, or technological.

Trade patterns also change dramatically. Globalization, once a defining feature of economic life, becomes fragile. With supply chains disrupted and long-distance transport unreliable, economies turn inward. Regional production replaces transcontinental dependency. Skills that were once devalued—craftsmanship, repair knowledge, small-scale farming—gain newfound importance. Local resilience becomes more valuable than global efficiency. Ironically, this shift mirrors pre-industrial economies, yet it integrates modern lessons about sustainability and resource limits.

A post-collapse economy also redefines labor. Without the rigid structures of corporate hierarchies or industrial specialization, people adopt fluid roles shaped by necessity rather than career aspiration. Cooperation becomes a pragmatic strategy, not a utopian ideal. Communities rely on collective problem-solving, reciprocal exchange, and shared responsibility. Work becomes meaningful not because it leads to wealth, but because it ensures survival and continuity. Social bonds strengthen because individuals understand that their well-being is intertwined with others.

Governance of economic life also transforms. Large institutions—central banks, multinational corporations, sprawling bureaucracies—lose relevance in the absence of stable global systems. Instead, smaller governance structures emerge: councils, assemblies, cooperatives, and local stewardship groups. These organizations manage resources collectively, enforce norms of fairness, and develop mechanisms for conflict resolution. Economic decision-making shifts closer to the ground, where consequences are immediate and visible.

Yet a post-collapse economy is not defined solely by scarcity. Over time, communities discover opportunities for renewal and innovation. Technologies previously used for mass consumption can be repurposed for resilience. Renewable energy systems—solar, wind, micro-hydropower—can decentralize power production. Permaculture and regenerative agriculture restore degraded ecosystems. Open-source knowledge allows communities to design tools, repair infrastructure, and build systems without relying on distant supply chains. In these environments, ingenuity becomes a primary economic asset.

However, the transition is not uniform. Some regions may rebuild quickly, leveraging remaining infrastructure and strong social cohesion. Others may fragment into enclaves with competing economic rules. Power struggles can emerge around scarce resources. Black markets may thrive where regulation disappears. A post-collapse world contains both opportunity and danger, collaboration and conflict. Economics becomes as much a study of human behavior as of resource allocation.

The central question is whether societies emerging from collapse repeat old patterns or invent new ones. If they cling to the logic of endless growth, competitive domination, and extraction, they may rebuild systems destined to fail again. But if they embrace regeneration, shared prosperity, and ecological limits, they may create more resilient forms of economic life. Collapse, painful as it is, can become a rare chance to reset foundational assumptions.

In essence, the economics of a post-collapse world revolves around three principles: **local resilience**, **ecological alignment**, and **distributed responsibility**. These principles do not reject complexity or innovation; they redefine the purpose of economic activity. Instead of serving markets, economies serve communities. Instead of chasing expansion, they cultivate stability. Instead of exploiting nature, they integrate with it.

A post-collapse world is not the end of economic life—but the beginning of an economic reckoning. It challenges humanity to design systems not for infinite growth, but for enduring survival, meaningful work, and a renewed relationship with the planet that sustains all value.

www.ingramcontent.com/pod-product-compliance
Lightning Source LLC
LaVergne TN
LVHW050918210926
848482LV00012B/485